# English Phrasal Verbs
## in Spanish

Kamal Khalaili and Blanca Marina

ANTONIO TLORES GUERRERO

Nelson

**Thomas Nelson and Sons Ltd**
Nelson House   Mayfield Road
Walton-on-Thames   Surrey
KT12 5PL   UK

51 York Place
Edinburgh
EH1 3JD   UK

**Thomas Nelson (Hong Kong) Ltd**
Toppan Building 10/F
22A Westlands Road
Quarry Bay   Hong Kong

© Kamal Khalaili and Blanca Marina 1983

First published by Hodder and Stoughton Ltd 1984.
Reprinted four times ISBN 0-340-33212-3

This edition published by Thomas Nelson and Sons Ltd 1991
ISBN 0-17-556099-4
NPN 9 8 7 6 5

Printed in Hong Kong.

# CONTENTS

# INTRODUCTION

The structure of English compared to Spanish can be quite different. Although in many ways grammatically simple, English does present considerable problems to the Spanish-speaking student, particularly in its colloquial use of verbs followed by prepositions or particles – the phrasal verb.

Everyday English has always relied heavily on such basic verbs as *put, take, get, make, bring, let,* and can form many combinations of these verbs with one or more prepositions or particles. These look deceptively easy to the foreigner at first sight, but their meanings can be radically different from what one might expect. Could anyone, for example, guess the meaning of such a phrase as *put up with,* purely from its constituent words?

The aim of this book is to illustrate the different meanings in context of a practical and representative selection of the most useful and widely used phrasal verbs – both in spoken and written English. It contains 44 sections, each devoted to a principal verb and the numerous combinations it can make with different prepositions or particles. Each phrasal verb is annotated grammatically* and accompanied by: a) a definition written in straightforward English, b) two examples to fix the context, c) a word-for-word translation of the definition in Spanish, and d) the equivalent Spanish word or phrase – which may not be a word-for-word translation of the verb or the definition – wherever one exists.

Completion exercises at the end of each section give student and teacher extra material to practise the correct and appropriate usage of these phrases. A key to these exercises is available to teachers from the publishers. Because a wide range of vocabulary is necessary to illustrate the full use of the phrasal verbs, an English-Spanish glossary has been provided at the back of the book. It contains about 400 items, each with a Spanish translation and a page reference indicating the point where the word first appears with a specific meaning in the text.

*English Phrasal Verbs in Spanish* makes no claim to be comprehensive or academically rigorous; it is designed rather to be of the maximum possible use, either in class or for private study, to Spanish students whose level ranges from «C» class to «Proficiency».

---

* See classification of verbs, p. 7.

# INTRODUCCIÓN

La estructura de la lengua inglesa, comparada a la de la española, puede ser muy diferente. Aunque el inglés es muchas veces muy simple gramaticalmente, puede presentar dificultades considerables al estudiante hispanohablante, concretamente en el uso coloquial de los verbos seguidos de preposición o de partículas; el llamado "phrasal verb" – verbo frasal.

El inglés corriente siempre se ha apoyado mucho en verbos básicos del tipo de Put, Take, Get, Make, Bring, Let, y puede formar muchas combinaciones con estos verbos y una o más preposiciones o partículas. Esto puede parecer muy fácil para un extranjero al principio, pero sus significados pueden ser radicalmente distintos de lo que uno espera. ¿ Se podría, por ej., adivinar lo que significa una expresión como "put up with" nada más que por el significado de las palabras que la forman?

La finalidad de esta obra es ilustrar los diferentes significados por medio de una selección práctica y representativa de los verbos frasales más útiles y más ampliamente usados en el inglés escrito y hablado. Contiene 44 secciones, cada una de las cuales está dedicada a un verbo principal y las diferentes combinaciones que puede hacer con distintas preposiciones y partículas. Cada verbo frasal está descrito gramaticalmente*y acompañado por: a) una definición escrita en inglés corriente, b) dos ejemplos ilustrativos, c) una traducción literal de la definición en español y d) la palabra o frase española, si es que existe, que puede no ser una traducción literal del verbo o de la definición.

Los ejercicios complementarios al final de cada sección dan al estudiante y al profesor material adicional para practicar el uso correcto y apropiado de estas expresiones. La editorial puede proporcionar a los profesores la solución a estos ejercicios.

Debido a la gran variedad de vocabulario que se necesita para ilustrar el uso completo de los verbos frasales, existe un glosario inglés-español al final del libro. Contiene unas 400 palabras, cada una con una traducción al español y una referencia de página que indica el lugar donde la palabra aparece por primera vez con un significado concreto en el texto.

"English Phrasal Verbs in Spanish" no pretende ser riguroso desde el punto de vista académico; más bien se ha hecho para que sea de la máxima utilidad en clase o privadamente, para los estudiantes españoles cuyo nivel sea entre First Certificate y "Proficiency".

---

* Ver la clasificación de los verbos en la pág. 7.

| LIST OF ABBREVIATIONS | | | LISTA DE ABREVIATURAS |
|---|---|---|---|
| *cf* | = | compare | = compare |
| *e.g.* | = | for example | = por ejemplo |
| *esp* | = | especially | = especialmente |
| *etc* | = | et cetera | = etcétera |
| *i.e.* | = | that is | = es decir; esto es; a saber |
| *imper* | = | imperative | = imperativo |
| *insep* | = | inseparable | = inseparable |
| *neg* | = | negative | = negativo |
| *opp* | = | opposite | = contrario |
| *pass* | = | passive | = voz pasiva |
| *sb* | = | somebody | = alguien |
| *sep* | = | separable | = separable |
| *sth* | = | something | = algo |
| *usu* | = | usually | = normalmente |
| *vi* | = | intransitive verb | = verbo intransitivo |
| *vt* | = | transitive verb | = verbo transitivo |

# CLASSIFICATION OF VERBS

*vi*: Verbs belonging to this category are normally inseparable, though sometimes adverbs may come between the verb and the particle, e.g. 'The procession passed by '/' The procession passed slowly by'.

*vt sep*: If the object of a verb belonging to this category is a noun, then the particle may precede or follow the noun, e.g. 'The man took off his hat' or 'The man took his hat off'. However, if the object is a pronoun (e.g. it, him, us) then the particle *must* follow it: 'The man took it off'.

*vt sep\**: Verbs belonging to this category must always be separated, regardless of whether the object is a noun or a pronoun, e.g. 'The sooner we get this job over the better' and 'The sooner we get it over the better'.

*vt insep*: Verbs belonging to this category must always be inseparable, that is to say the particle(s) must follow the verb immediately, regardless of whether the object is a noun or a pronoun, e.g. 'The police are looking into the case'/'The police are looking into it' and 'I look forward to meeting John'/'I look forward to meeting him'.

---

\*All English words in the text marked with an asterisk appear, with a translation into Spanish, in the English-Spanish glossary at the back of the book.

Todas las palabras inglesas marcadas en el texto con un asterisco aparecen con una traducción al español en el glosario inglés-español al final del libro.

# AGREE

**agree to**
*vt insep*

accept; consent to
*acceder a; aceptar; aprobar; consentir*

I'm pleased to hear that you have finally *agreed to* our proposals*.
Her parents just won't *agree to* her marrying a foreigner.


**agree (up)on**
*vt insep*

be unanimous about
*convenir en; ponerse de acuerdo*

Why can't you two ever *agree on* anything?
They agreed on the course of action to be taken.
Has the date for the next meeting been *agreed upon* yet?


**agree with**
1 *vt insep*

have the same opinion as
*estar de acuerdo*

I *agree with* everything you have said so far.
Many people did not *agree with* the speaker on the last point he made.
I'm afraid I can't *agree with* you in this matter.


**agree with**
2 *vt insep*

tally with; correspond with
*concordar con; cuadrar con*

His story doesn't quite *agree with* that of the other witness*, does it?


**agree with**
3 *vt insep*

approve of
*estar de acuerdo con; aprobar*

Do you *agree with* nudity* on the stage?
I don't *agree with* spoiling children too much.


**agree with**
4 *vt insep*

suit sb.'s health, temperament, etc.
*convenir; sentar bien (o mal) a uno*

Indian food does not *agree with* me.
The tropical* climate does not *agree with* David.

9

Fill in the blank spaces with the correct propositions:

1 The manager agreed ... my request for a day off.
2 Oh, there is no doubt about that; I entirely agree ... you.
3 We could not agree ... a price for the house.
4 Garlic does not agree ... my husband.
5 The engineers will call off their strike if the management agrees ... their demands.
6 Do you agree ... women smoking in the street?
7 Have you agreed ... the terms of the contract yet?

# BACK

**back away**
*vi*

retreat; move back
*moverse hacia atrás; recular*

She *backed away* nervously at the sight of the snake.
The child *backed away* from the angry dog.

**back down**
*vi*

abandon an opinion, a claim, etc.
*ceder; dar marcha atrás; rajarse*

At first he refused to comply* with the court order, but *backed down* when he realized he could be penalized* heavily.
He won't *back down* unless he is forced to do so.

**back on to**
*vt insep*

overlook from the back
*dar a un sitio por la parte trasera*

Their house *backs on to* Hyde Park.
The shop *backs on to* a railway station.

**back out**
*vi*

withdraw (from a promise, bargain, etc.)
*volverse atrás; romper (un acuerdo/un contrato)*

It's too late to *back out* now; I'm afraid we shall have to go through with it.
He *backed out* of the agreement, because he knew the others would not abide* by it.

| | |
|---|---|
| **back up** | give support to |
| *vt sep* | *(a) apoyar; respaldar: (b) corroborar; confirmar* |

If I protest against the decision, will you *back* me *up*?
The police were unwilling to believe her story, because she had no evidence* to *back* it *up*.

*EXERCISE 2*

Fill in the blank spaces with the correct prepositions or particles:

1 He always backs his friends . . . when they are in trouble.
2 They have backed . . . . . . the bargain at the last minute.
3 The house backs . . . . . . the football stadium.
4 He was quite determined to fight for it, but now he seems to have backed . . .
5 The frightened horses backed . . . from the tiger.

# BE

| | |
|---|---|
| **be about to** | be on the point of |
| *vi* | *estar a punto de* |

The teacher *was about to* start the lesson when I came in.
The ceremony *is about to* finish.

| | |
|---|---|
| **be after** | want; seek |
| *vt insep* | *querer; pretender* |

He doesn't really love her; he's only *after* her money.
What *are* you *after*? Just tell me plainly.

| | |
|---|---|
| **be along** | come; arrive |
| *vi* | *venir; llegar* |

The doctor will *be along* any minute now.
Tell Mr Hopkins I'll *be along* in a moment.

| | |
|---|---|
| **be away** | be absent (from home, office, etc.) |
| *vi* | *estar ausente; estar fuera* |

I'm afraid Mrs Thompson *is away* on holiday this week.
He's *away* from the office and won't be back till Thursday.

11

**be back**
  *vi*

return; have returned
*regresar; volver*

The manager is out for lunch. He'*ll be back* in an hour or so.
I'*ll be back* as soon as I can.

**be behind**
  *vi, vt insep*

be late; be delayed
*estar atrasado; ir atrasado en/con respeto a*

They *were* well *behind* with the schedule*.
We *are* all *behind* with our payments.
Suzy *is behind* the rest of the girls in her studies.

**be down**
  *vi*

be depressed; be dejected
*estar abatido; estar desalentado o deprimido*

Jonathan *is* a bit *down* because he failed his driving test.

**be down on**
  *vt insep*

be prejudiced against; be critical of
*tener antipatía a; estar predispuesto en contra de*

All the critics* seem *to be down on* that author.
She *has been down on* him ever since he complained about her to the boss.

**be for**
  *vt insep*

be in favour of
*ser partidario de; apoyar; estar a favor de*

I'*m for* the Republicans, but he'*s for* the Democrats.
*Are* you *for* or against the abolition* of the death* penalty?

**be in**
  *vi*

be at home, in one's office, etc.
*estar; estar en casa/en la oficina*

I'd like to see Dr. Bentley. *Is* he *in*?
Yes, he'*s in*, but I'm afraid he's rather busy at the moment.

**be off**
  1 *vi*

go; leave
*irse; marcharse*

I'm sorry I can't keep the appointment with you; I'*m off* to Paris tomorrow.

We'd better *be off* before it gets dark.
I must *be off* now; it's getting rather late.

**be off**
2 *vi*

be cancelled
*suspenderse; anularse*

The meeting which was scheduled for tomorrow *is off*.
The match *is off* once again.

**be off**
3 *vi*

have gone bad
*estar pasado; estar en mal estado*

The fish you've sold me *is off*.
Don't eat that steak; it's slightly *off*.

**be on**
1 *vi*

(of films etc.) be showing
*poner (en el cine); representar (en el teatro)*

I wonder what film *is on* at the Imperial Cinema.
'Macbeth' *was on* at the Royal Theatre only last week.

**be on**
2 *vi*

be going to take place
*tener lugar; celebrarse*

The meeting *is on* again in spite of all the setbacks.

**be out**
1 *vi*

be out of the house, office, etc.
*estar fuera (de casa/de la oficina)*

The manager *is out* for lunch, but he'll be back at one
o'clock.

**be out**
2 *vi*

be inaccurate; be wrong
*equivocarse; hacer mal (un cálculo)*

The doctor *was* way *out* in his diagnosis*.
They *were* far *out* in their calculations.

**be out**
3 *vi*

be on strike
*estar en huelga*

The miners *are out* again.
Most of the workers at that factory *were out* during
the last two weeks.

| | |
|---|---|
| **be out of**<br>*vt insep* | have no more of<br>*no tener provisiones; quedarse sin (gasolina, etc.)*<br><br>We *are out of* bread. Will you go and buy some?<br>The shops *are* completely *out of* milk. |
| **be out to**<br>*vi* | be determined to<br>*estar decidido a*<br><br>Robin *is* all *out to* pass his final examinations.<br>The government *is out to* curb inflation*. |
| **be over**<br>*vi* | be finished; be ended<br>*terminarse; acabarse*<br><br>The present heat wave is expected *to be over* soon.<br>Well, it's all *over* now. You needn't worry about it any longer. |
| **be through**<br>*vi* | reach the end of a relationship<br>*terminar (las relaciones)*<br><br>I won't put up with his bad temper any longer. We're *through*. |
| **be through with**<br>*vt insep* | be finished with<br>*acabar con; terminar con*<br><br>I'll join you as soon as I'm *through with* these letters.<br>I don't know when he'll *be through with* that job. |
| **be up**<br>1 *vi* | be out of bed<br>*estar levantado*<br><br>The children *were up* at five this morning.<br>He must *be up* by now. It's nearly twelve o'clock. |
| **be up**<br>2 *vi* | (of time) expire; be finished<br>*terminar; expirar (un plazo)*<br><br>Time's *up*, gentlemen!<br>She managed to answer all the questions before the time *was up*. |

14

| **be up to** | be capable of |
|---|---|
| 1 *vt insep* | *ser capaz de; tener fuerzas para hacer* |

He has made a terrible mess of the job. I'm afraid he *is* not *up to* it.
Whcn shc was younger, she *was up to* walking ten miles a day.

| **be up to** | be equal to |
|---|---|
| 2 *vt insep* | *estar a la altura de; estar conforme a un debido nivel* |

Your work *is* not *up to* the required standard.

| **be up to** | be depending on |
|---|---|
| 3 *vt insep* | *(a) depender de uno; (b) incumbir a uno* |

You can either punish him or let him off. It's entirely *up to* you.
It's not *up to* me to decide on these matters.

| **be up to** | be engaged in (some mischievous act) |
|---|---|
| 4 *vt insep* | *preparar; maquinar; tramar (algo malo)* |

These boys *are* always *up to* mischief*.
Don't trust that fellow; I tell you he *is up to* no good.


*EXERCISE 3*

Fill in the blank spaces with the correct prepositions or particles:

1 Philip has been ill for well over a month. He must be ... with his studies by now.
2 The concert was ... at eleven o'clock.
3 What have you been ......? I haven't seen you for ages.
4 I'm ...... money at the moment. Will you lend me a few pounds?
5 What play is ... at the Shakespeare Theatre?
6 The delegation* is ... to Russia on a highly important mission.
7 We thought we would need ten bottles of wine for the party, but we were ... in our estimate*. In fact we needed seven more.
8 The patient's condition has improved considerably, but he is not ... ... going out yet.
9 He has just gone to the shop to buy a few things, and will be ... in half an hour.
10 I was just ...... have my dinner when the telephone rang.
11 We are not going to do the show after all; it's ....

12 The choice is not entirely ...... me, I'm afraid. I'll have to consult my partner.
13 We should be ...... this job by Friday at the latest.
14 She was ... early this morning to do the packing.
15 You don't seem to be fond of Stuart. You're always ...... him.

# BEAR

**bear down (up)on**
*vt insep*

move swiftly and menacingly towards
*avanzar amenazadoramente hacia*

A lion *was bearing down upon* its helpless prey* at lightning speed.
The big ship *bore down on* our small boat.


**bear out**
*vt sep*

confirm; support
*confirmar; corroborar*

This story of yours *bears out* his innocence beyond all doubt.
Is there anyone who can *bear* you *out* on this?
My friend Hill *will bear out* everything I have told you.


**bear up**
*vi*

remain strong under adversity or affliction
*sobreponerse a*

It must be very hard for her *to bear up* against the death of her only child.
I know how disappointed you must be feeling, but do try *to bear up*, won't you?


**bear (up)on**
*vt insep*

relate to; affect
*tener que ver con; referirse a*

How *does* this *bear on* the subject we are discussing?
These are major issues that directly *bear upon* the security of the state.

16

| **bear with** | tolerate; be patient with |
|---|---|
| *vt insep* | *soportar; aguantar; tener paciencia con* |

I can't *bear with* his foul temper any longer.
If you *will bear with* me for a few more minutes, I will show you what I mean.
'*Bear with* me;
My heart is in the coffin there with Caesar,
And I must pause till it come back to me.'

Shakespeare, *Julius Caesar*

*EXERCISE 4*

Fill in the blank spaces with the correct prepositions or particles:

1 Your remark doesn't bear . . . the matter at issue, I'm afraid.
2 The evidence you have now bears . . . my theory.
3 How is she bearing . . . after her bereavement*?
4 Bear . . . me while I find the letter.
5 The headmistress bore . . . . . . the frightened girls.
6 I find it impossible to bear . . . his impudence*.
7 What you are telling me now bears . . . my suspicions.

# BLOW

| **blow in(to)** | arrive unexpectedly |
|---|---|
| *vi, vt insep* | *entrar/llegar inesperadamente* |

John *blew in* last night to tell us about his promotion*.
Guess who's just *blown into* my office.

| **blow out** | be extinguished; extinguish |
|---|---|
| *vi, vt sep* | *apagar soplando; apagarse* |

The lamp *will blow out* if you don't shut that door.
The little girl was anxious *to blow out* the candles on her birthday cake.

| **blow over** | subside; be forgotten |
|---|---|
| *vi* | *(a) (de una tormenta) pasar; (b) no tener consequencias; pasar* |

The crew of the ship were greatly relieved when the storm finally *blew over*.
There is no need to worry about it; the whole thing *will* soon *blow over*.

17

| | | |
|---|---|---|
| **blow up**<br>1 *vi* | (of a storm etc.) develop<br>*(de una tormenta) estallar; sobrevenir* | |

If a storm were suddenly *to blow up*, our boat would capsize*.

| | |
|---|---|
| **blow up**<br>2 *vi* | lose one's temper<br>*reventar; estallar (de ira)* |

When the soldier refused to carry out his orders, the sergeant* just *blew up*.
I'm sorry I *blew up* at you yesterday; I was in a rather bad mood.

| | |
|---|---|
| **blow up**<br>3 *vi, vt sep* | (cause to) explode<br>*estallar (una bomba); hacer saltar; volar* |

The bomb *blew up*, killing five people.
The commandos* *blew* the bridge *up* and fled unharmed.
A lot of oil refineries* *were blown up* during the last war.

| | |
|---|---|
| **blow up**<br>4 *vt sep* | inflate; fill with air<br>*hinchar; inflar* |

The child kept *blowing up* the balloon till it burst.
Before you go on the road, make sure your tyres *are* properly *blown up*.

| | |
|---|---|
| **blow up**<br>5 *vt sep* | reprimand; scold<br>*echar una bronca a uno; reñir* |

The teacher *blew* me *up* for arriving late this morning.

| | |
|---|---|
| **blow up**<br>6 *vt sep* | enlarge<br>*ampliar* |

Get someone *to blow up* these photographs, please.
I'd like you *to blow up* this part of the picture as much as you can.


## EXERCISE 5

Use synonyms* in place of the underlined phrasal verbs:

1 The mother <u>blew</u> her son <u>up</u> for answering her back.

18

2 The much-talked-about scandal* finally <u>blew over</u>.
3 Who do you think <u>blew in</u> to see me this morning?
4 We have enough explosives to <u>blow up</u> the entire building.
5 I thought I'd just <u>blow in</u> to see how you are getting on with your work.
6 The wind <u>blew</u> the light <u>out</u>.
7 He just <u>blew up</u> when I told him I'd forgotten to post the letter.
8 She liked the picture and wanted to have it <u>blown up</u>.

# BREAK

**break away**      secede
1 *vi*              *separarse de*

Several members of the Labour Party *have broken away* in protest against its nationalization* policy.

**break away**      renounce; abandon
2 *vi*              *romper con; renunciar*

It's not always easy *to break away* from bad company. He *has broken away* from his family and decided to settle in Canada.

**break away**      free oneself from
3 *vi*              *escaparse de; evadirse de*

The prisoner managed *to break away* from his guards.

**break down**      cease to function
1 *vi*              *estropearse; averiarse*

My car *has broken down* again and badly needs servicing. These machines *will break down* if they are left without proper maintenance*.

**break down**      be discontinued
2 *vi*              *interrumpirse; suspender (negociaciones, etc)*

The negotiations* *broke down* and may not be resumed* until the autumn.

| | |
|---|---|
| **break down**<br>3 *vi* | break into tears; collapse<br>*echarse a llorar; destrozarse*<br><br>On hearing of her husband's death she *broke down.*<br>His health *has broken down* from overwork and malnutrition*. |
| **break down**<br>4 *vt sep* | destroy by breaking<br>*derribar; echar abajo*<br><br>I'm going *to break down* the door if you won't let me in. |
| **break down**<br>5 *vt sep* | classify<br>*analizar; descomponer*<br><br>If you *break* these statistics* *down,* you'll see that 50% of those unemployed are under the age of twenty. |
| **break in**<br>1 *vt sep* | train (a horse etc.)<br>*domar (un caballo, etc)*<br><br>It would be foolish of you to try to ride that vicious horse before it *is* safely *broken in.* |
| **break in**<br>2 *vi* | interrupt<br>*interrumpir; cortar*<br><br>A few hecklers* *broke in* as the minister was speaking. |
| **break in(to)**<br>1 *vi, vt insep* | force entry into<br>*forzar una entrada*<br><br>Thieves *broke in* and ransacked* the house.<br>Burglars* *broke into* the museum and stole eight priceless paintings. |
| **break into**<br>2 *vt insep* | begin suddenly<br>*empezar a; echarse a (correr, etc)*<br><br>On hearing the funny joke everyone *broke into* laughter.<br>As they boarded the bus, the boys *broke into* song. |

| | |
|---|---|
| **break off**<br>1 *vi* | stop for a rest or break<br>*pararse; suspender (el trabajo, etc)* |
| | The workers *broke off* for lunch at twelve.<br>Let us *break off* for just a few minutes. |
| **break off**<br>2 *vt sep* | terminate; sever<br>*romper (las relaciones, etc)* |
| | Unable to settle their differences, they decided *to break off* their engagement.<br>Many African countries *have broken off* diplomatic relations with Israel. |
| **break off**<br>3 *vt sep* | detach<br>*separar; partir* |
| | The child *broke off* a piece of chocolate and gave it to his sister. |
| **break out**<br>1 *vi* | start suddenly<br>*estallar; declararse (la guerra, una epidemia)* |
| | The First World War *broke out* in 1914.<br>Fire *broke out* in the hotel and destroyed it completely.<br>A new epidemic* of cholera* *has broken out*. |
| **break out**<br>2 *vi* | escape (from a place)<br>*evadirse; escaparse* |
| | If he tries *to break out* shoot him.<br>Three men *broke out* of this prison last week. |
| **break through**<br>*vi, vt insep* | penetrate<br>*penetrar (las líneas enemigas)* |
| | After two weeks of dogged* fighting, our troops *broke through* (the enemy's lines). |
| **break up**<br>1 *vi* | disband (at the end of term)<br>*(de un colegio) cerrarse; terminar* |
| | The school *breaks up* on June 18th.<br>When *do* you *break up* for the Christmas holidays? |

| **break up** | break into pieces |
|---|---|
| 2 *vi, vt sep* | *hacerse pedazos; romperse* |

The ship *broke up* on the rocks.
We *broke up* the old car and sold it as scrap.

| **break up** | disperse; scatter |
|---|---|
| 3 *vi, vt sep* | *dispersar, disolver; dispersarse* |

The meeting *broke up* at about eleven.
The police used tear-gas* *to break up* the demonstration.

| **break up** | (of a couple) part |
|---|---|
| 4 *vi* | *(de esposos) separarse* |

I thought they were very happy together. Why *did* they *break up*?
Peter and Lily *broke up* nearly a year ago.


*EXERCISE 6*

Fill in the blank spaces with the correct prepositions or particles:

1 They suddenly broke ... their conversation when they saw me coming.
2 When do you break ... for Easter*?
3 I want you to break ... these figures and tell me how much we have spent on housing schemes* alone.
4 When did the Second World War break ... ?
5 The bus broke ... on the way to Glasgow, and we were stranded there for hours.
6 Will you please stop breaking ... while I'm talking!
7 When he learnt of his son's tragic death, the old man broke ... and cried.
8 During the recent riots* many department stores were broken ... and looted*.
9 Fifty people were killed when a fire broke ... in the building.
10 During the American Civil War, eleven states broke ... to form the Southern Confederacy.
11 The prisoner broke ... of gaol by climbing a nine-foot wall.
12 Judith has broken ... her engagement to Anthony.
13 If we don't break ... the fight, someone will get hurt.
14 I tied the horse to a tree, but he managed to break ....
15 Someone broke ... my office and stole the papers.

# BRING

**bring about**
*vt sep*

cause to happen
*ocasionar; producir*

We sincerely hope that these talks *will bring about* a reconciliation\* between the two countries.
It was the Watergate affair that *brought about* the downfall of Richard Nixon.

**bring back**
1 *vt sep*

return
*devolver*

I'll lend you my car provided you *bring* it *back* tomorrow.

**bring back**
2 *vt insep*

reintroduce
*introducir de nuevo; reinstaurar*

A lot of M.P.'s\* are clearly in favour of *bringing back* capital\* punishment.

**bring back**
3 *vt sep*

recall to the mind; remind one of
*recordar; hacer pensar en; traer (buenos recuerdos)*

That old song *brought back* happy memories to her.
It's amazing how a few words can *bring* it all *back*.

**bring down**
1 *vt sep*

shoot down (a plane)
*derribar; abatir*

Twenty of the enemy's fighter aircraft *have been brought down* by ground-to-air missiles\*.

**bring down**
2 *vt sep*

cause to fall
*derribar; hacer caer (la monarquía, el gobierno)*

These unpopular measures\* could *bring* the government *down*.

**bring down**
3 *vt sep*

reduce; lower (a price)
*rebajar; bajar*

The government intends *to bring* the price of bread *down* to fifteen pence a loaf.

23

**bring forth**
*vt insep*

produce; yield
*producir; dar*

If the drought* continues to persist, the fruit-trees *will bring forth* nothing.
I wonder what the future *will bring forth.*

**bring forward**
1 *vt sep*

raise; propose for discussion
*proponer; presentar*

I feel we ought *to bring forward* this proposal at the next meeting of the Council.

**bring forward**
2 *vt sep*

make earlier
*adelantar; anticipar*

The committee has decided *to bring forward* the date of the conference to next May.
In view of this emergency*, our meeting is *to be brought forward* from the 20th to the 13th April.

**bring in**
1 *vt sep*

introduce (a reform, a Bill*, etc.)
*presentar (un proyecto de ley, etc)*

The Prime Minister intends *to bring in* major industrial reforms*.
The government is expected *to bring in* a Bill on road safety shortly.

**bring in**
2 *vt sep*

yield; produce
*producir; rendir (ganancia)*

His investments* in the various companies *bring* him *in* a total of £1000 a year.

**bring in**
3 *vt insep*

pronounce (a verdict)
*pronunciar (una sentencia)*

The jury* *brought in* a verdict* of 'not guilty'.
To the great relief of the accused, a verdict of 'not guilty' *was brought in.*

**bring off**
1 *vt sep*

bring to a successful conclusion
*lograr; conseguir*

The scheme will meet with strong opposition, but we believe we can *bring* it *off* eventually.

24

| | |
|---|---|
| **bring off**<br>2 *vt sep* | rescue<br>*salvar; rescatar* |

The coastguard patrol *brought off* the crew of the sinking ship.
All passengers *were brought off* by helicopters.

| | |
|---|---|
| **bring on**<br>*vt sep* | cause; induce<br>*causar; ocasionar* |

Such cold and extremely damp weather often *brings on* influenza.
Her attack of pneumonia* *was brought on* by the severe winter and lack of adequate heating at home.

| | |
|---|---|
| **bring out**<br>1 *vt sep* | show; reveal; expose<br>*sacar a luz; revelar; explicar (la diferencia entre)* |

The teacher gave sentences *to bring out* the difference between 'destiny'* and 'destination'*.
The inquiry may well *bring out* surprising things about the illicit* practices of some police officers.

| | |
|---|---|
| **bring out**<br>2 *vt sep* | publish (see *come out* (3))<br>*sacar; poner en venta; publicar* |

The publishers *have* just *brought out* a new edition of their popular cookery book.
His new novel *will be brought out* in a month's time.

| | |
|---|---|
| **bring over**<br>*vt sep* | convince; convert<br>*convencer; persuadirle a uno a aceptar algo* |

We may be able *to bring* him *over* to our side, but it won't be easy.

| | |
|---|---|
| **bring round**<br>1 *vt sep** | carry or take (to a certain place)<br>*traer (a algun sitio)* |

Tell the chauffeur *to bring* the car *round* to the front door.
*Bring* her *round* to see me one evening, won't you?

* Phrasal verbs which are marked *sep** must always be separated from their particles.

**bring round**
2 *vt sep\**

restore to consciousness
*hacer volver en sí; hacer recobrarse*

We *brought* him *round* by splashing cold water on his face.
With the help of a doctor, it shouldn't take long *to bring* the young lady *round.*

**bring round**
3 *vt sep\**

persuade; convert
*convencer; persuadirle a uno aceptar algo*

At first he was strongly opposed to the idea, but I managed *to bring* him *round* in the end.
After a rather lengthy argument he *was brought round* to my point of view.

**bring through**
*vt sep\**

save (a sick person)
*salvar la vida a uno*

She was critically ill in hospital, but good doctors *brought* her *through.*
Even the best medical treatment failed *to bring* the patient *through* his illness.

**bring to**
*vt sep\**

= BRING ROUND (2)

**bring under**
*vt sep\**

subdue; control
*dominar; someter a*

The rebels must *be brought under* at all costs.
Germany *was brought under* Fascist rule.

**bring up**
1 *vt sep*

rear; raise
*criar; educar*

To *bring up* a family of six must cost a lot of money these days.
Those children *are* very badly *brought up.*
He *was brought up* to obey his elders and betters.

**bring up**
2 *vt sep*

vomit
*vomitar*

She was very ill and *brought up* everything she had eaten.
The baby keeps *bringing up* her food.

| **bring up** | raise; mention |
|---|---|
| 3 *vt sep* | *plantear (un problema); mencionar* |

He promised *to bring* the matter *up* at the next committee\* meeting.
Several interesting points *were brought up* in the course of the discussion.


*EXERCISE 7*

A   Use synonyms in place of the underlined phrasal verbs:

1   New measures are being <u>brought in</u> to deal with tax\* evasion.
2   I wish you'd stop <u>bringing up</u> this subject every time I see you.
3   The sudden outbreak of cholera has been <u>brought about</u> by the recent floods.
4   What verdict did the jury <u>bring in</u>?
5   When his mother died, Charles Dickens was <u>brought up</u> by his sister.
6   Living in such squalid\* conditions <u>brings on</u> all kinds of diseases.
7   <u>Bring</u> the laundry <u>round</u> to my house.
8   I think they ought to <u>bring back</u> corporal\* punishment.
9   Owing to the surplus\* of butter its price has been <u>brought down</u> considerably.
10  That publishing firm has <u>brought out</u> a new science encyclopaedia\*.


B   Fill in the blank spaces with the correct prepositions or particles. In some examples more than one answer is possible:

1   It shouldn't be difficult to bring him ... to our way of thinking.
2   He was badly injured in a car accident, but special attention and good nursing brought him ....
3   A reconnaissance\* plane was brought ... by anti-aircraft artillery\*.
4   These new products bring ... a good deal of money.
5   We are bringing ... his collection of essays next month.
6   New land is being brought ... cultivation\*.
7   She fainted in a crowded bus, but was quickly brought ... with a brandy.
8   Please bring the book ... to me when you've finished with it.
9   They have brought ... yet another important business deal.
10  The MP was so concerned about the matter that he intended to bring it ... in Parliament.

# CALL

**call back**
1 *vi, vt sep*

telephone back
*volver a llamar (por teléfono)*

The operator *called back* while you were out.
I'*ll call* you *back* as soon as I know the results.

**call back**
2 *vt sep*

recall; summon to return
*llamar; hacer volver*

The ambassador *has been called back* for urgent consultations* with his government.

**call for**
1 *vt insep*

require; demand
*reclamar; exigir*

Such delicate matters *call for* considerable tact* and skill.
The good news *calls for* a celebration.
The Home* Secretary *is calling for* an inquiry* into allegations* of corruption* in the police department.

**call for**
2 *vt insep*

go and fetch
*venir a recoger*

I'*ll call for* you at your office at, say, four o'clock.
He said he *would call for* his car tomorrow afternoon.

**call forth**
*vt insep*

bring into action; provoke
*provocar; sacar*

This crisis *has called forth* all his energy.
The government's decision *has called forth* angry protests from Labour back-benchers*.

**call in**
1 *vt sep*

summon to a place
*llamar; pedir la ayuda de*

We can't afford *to call in* a technician every time the TV set breaks down.
She *has called* her lawyer *in* and instructed him to draw up a new will*.

| | |
|---|---|
| **call in**<br>2 *vt sep* | request the return of<br>*retirar; pedir el pago inmediato de (una deuda)*<br><br>The manufacturers *have called in* all the defective* models and corrected them.<br>The firm will soon start *calling* their debts *in*. |
| **call off**<br>*vt sep* | cancel; abandon<br>*abandonar; suspender; anular*<br><br>We had *to call off* the procession* because of the bad weather.<br>They *called* the deal *off* at the very last minute.<br>The search for the missing aircraft *was* finally *called off*. |
| **call out**<br>1 *vt sep* | announce in a loud voice<br>*(a) anunciar (o decir) en voz alta; (b) pasar la lista de*<br><br>Will you please keep quiet while I *call out* the results.<br>The teacher *called out* the names of the pupils before starting the lesson. |
| **call out**<br>2 *vt sep* | summon to strike<br>*llamar a la huelga*<br><br>Following their abortive* talks with the government, the Union* officials decided *to call* the workers *out*. |
| **call up**<br>1 *vt sep* | telephone; ring up<br>*llamar (por teléfono)*<br><br>I'*ll call* you *up* as soon as I get there.<br>David *called* me *up* last night and told me about the accident. |
| **call up**<br>2 *vt sep* | summon for military service<br>*llamar al servicio militar*<br><br>The army *is calling up* reservists* in case of renewed hostilities.<br>He *was called up* just before the outbreak of the war. |

| call (up)on | visit briefly |
|---|---|
| 1 *vt insep* | *ir a ver; hacer una visita a* |

While I was in London I *called on* aunt Felicity.
I will *call on* you at about five, if that is convenient for you.

| call (up)on | invite; request |
|---|---|
| 2 *vt insep* | *ceder la palabra a; invitar a hablar* |

I will now *call on* Mr Jones to deliver his speech.
The secretary was *called upon* to read the minutes* of the meeting.


*EXERCISE 8*

Fill in the blank spaces with the correct prepositions or particles:

1 The football pitch* was so wet that the referee decided to call ... the match.
2 Here is my phone number; you can call me ... any time between 8 am and 4 pm.
3 The library is calling ... all the books that are overdue*.
4 When I went to Italy last year I called ... my friends in Rome.
5 You look very ill. Shall I call ... a doctor?
6 He has been called ... from Berlin to supervise the operation.
7 This alarming situation calls ... immediate action.
8 She stepped forward to receive her prize when her name was called ...
9 Harry is calling ... me at seven to take me to the pictures.
10 He was never called ... to the army because of his poor healtn.


# CARRY

| carry away | (*usu. pass.*) deprive of self-control |
|---|---|
| *vt sep* | *entusiasmarse (demasiado); dejarse llevar por* |

The speaker got *carried away* by his enthusiasm*.
She was so *carried away* by her emotions that she did not know what she was saying.
We haven't won the game yet, so don't get *carried away*.

| | |
|---|---|
| **carry forward**<br>*vt sep* | transfer (an amount etc.) to the next column, page, etc.<br>*pasar a cuenta nueva* |

The book-keeper* *carried* the figures *forward* to the next page.
At the end of the month all balances *are carried forward.*

| | |
|---|---|
| **carry off**<br>1 *vt sep** | handle<br>*llevar a cabo* |

She had a difficult part to play, but she *carried* it *off* extremely well.

| | |
|---|---|
| **carry off**<br>2 *vt sep* | win (a prize etc.)<br>*ganar (un premio)* |

The Russian athletes* *carried off* most of the gold medals at the last Olympic Games.
Who do you think *will carry off* the first prize in tomorrow's competition*?

| | |
|---|---|
| **carry on**<br>1 *vi* | continue; proceed<br>*seguir; continuar* |

She was asked to stop talking and *carry on* with her work.
Sorry if I interrupted you. Please *carry on*!
I tried to start a conversation with him, but he just ignored me and *carried on* reading his paper.

| | |
|---|---|
| **carry on**<br>2 *vi* | have an affair (with)<br>*entenderse con* |

They *had been carrying on* for quite a while, but managed to keep it secret.
All the neighbours know that his wife *is carrying on* with the lodger*.

| | |
|---|---|
| **carry on**<br>3 *vi* | behave<br>*portarse; seguir (haciendo algo)* |

If you *carry on* in that way, you'll get yourself a bad name.

31

| | |
|---|---|
| **carry on**<br>4 *vt insep* | manage (a business); hold (a conversation)<br>*(a) tener, ser dueño de (un negocio); (b) tener (una conversación)* |

His father *carries on* a textile business in the centre of town.
It's impossible *to carry on* any kind of conversation in this terrible noise.

| | |
|---|---|
| **carry out**<br>*vt insep* | execute; perform<br>*cumplir (una promesa, etc); llevar a cabo* |

A plan such as this would be very costly *to carry out*.
They *did* not *carry out* their promise to help us.
The doctor's orders will have *to be carried out* to the letter*.

| | |
|---|---|
| **carry through**<br>1 *vt sep* | accomplish; complete<br>*llevar a cabo* |

We did not have enough capital* *to carry* the scheme *through*.
The enterprise* *was carried through* in spite of all the setbacks.

| | |
|---|---|
| **carry through**<br>2 *vt sep*** | help through a difficult period<br>*sostener; mantener* |

His dogged* determination did not fail *to carry* him *through*.
They prayed to God *to carry* them *through* their ordeal*.

*EXERCISE 9*

Fill in the blank spaces with the correct particles:

1 An extensive search for the missing aeroplane is being carried ... by rescue teams.
2 The teacher read the first paragraph and then asked Helen to carry ....
3 If we are to win the war, our struggle must be carried ... to the end.
4 She suspected that her husband was carrying ... with the woman next door.
5 Every time we discuss our holiday plans, my wife just gets carried ....
6 The Belgian team carried ... all the trophies* at the show-jumping event.
7 Their son carries ... the business of a hotelier at a seaside resort*.
8 He carried ... like a child at the party.

# CATCH

**catch on**
1 *vi*

become popular
*hacerse popular; tener éxito*

The latest Paris fashions *have caught on* rapidly everywhere in Europe.
This kind of song is likely *to catch on* with the younger generation.

**catch on**
2 *vi*

understand; comprehend
*comprender; caer en la cuenta*

She is a very shrewd* woman. Trust her *to catch on* to what they are doing.

**catch out**
*vt sep**

trap; trick
*sorprender; coger en una trampa*

Are you trying *to catch* me *out* with these smart questions of yours?
You'd better be careful with him, or he'*ll catch* you *out.*

**catch up**
**(with)**
*vi, vt sep**

draw level with
*alcanzar; emparejarse a uno*

He was unable *to catch up* with the rest of the class, because of his repeated absence from school.
We have to run faster, or they'*ll* soon *catch* us *up.*

*EXERCISE 10*

Fill in the blank spaces with the correct particles:

1 Vera has been ill for some time now. It'll take her a few weeks to catch ... with her work.
2 These revolutionary ideas will never catch ... in a conservative* society such as ours.
3 They left only a few minutes ago, but if you hurry you should be able to catch ... with them.
4 Do you think this new style will ever catch ... ?
5 It's no good trying to catch me .... I know all your little tricks.
6 He is no fool. Actually he's very quick at catching ....

# CLEAR

**clear away**
1 *vi*

disappear; vanish
*desvanecer; desaparecer*

The clouds are beginning *to clear away*.
The mist *will have cleared away* by the time we get there.

**clear away**
2 *vt sep*

remove
*quitar (escombros, etc)*

When we had finished eating, the waitress *cleared away* the dirty plates.
The workers started *clearing* the debris* *away* shortly after the explosion.

**clear off**
1 *vi*

go away
*irse; largarse*

You'd better *clear off* before my father arrives.
I don't want your help, so *clear off*!
*Clear off*, the lot of you!

**clear off**
2 *vt sep*

get rid of; dispose of
*liquidar (una deuda, etc); deshacerse de*

He had accumulated* so many debts that he could not *clear* them *off*.
If you intend *to clear off* this old stock you'll have to sell it cheaply.

**clear out**
1 *vi*

= CLEAR OFF (1)

**clear out**
2 *vt sep*

clean out; empty
*vaciar; limpiar*

She *cleared out* one of the cupboards to let her room-mate use it.

**clear out**
3 *vt sep*

throw out; expel
*echar (a la calle)*

Go and *clear* those kids *out* of my room.
He *was cleared out* of the pub for causing a disturbance.

| | |
|---|---|
| **clear up**<br>1 *vi* | (of the weather) become clear<br>*despejarse (el tiempo)* |

I hope the weather *will* soon *clear up.*
It's rather cloudy now, but it may *clear up* later in the day.

| | |
|---|---|
| **clear up**<br>2 *vt sep* | make tidy; remove<br>*arreglar; poner en orden* |

She spent all morning *clearing up* the children's playroom.
After the party, some guests stayed behind to help *clear up* the mess.

| | |
|---|---|
| **clear up**<br>3 *vt sep* | make clear, solve<br>*resolver; aclarar* |

Before we go any further, I'd like *to clear up* this matter once and for all.
The mystery of the kidnapped* heiress* *was* never *cleared up.*

*EXERCISE 11*

Use synonyms in place of the underlined phrasal verbs:

1 The gang <u>cleared off</u> when they saw the police coming.
2 We were so glad to see the clouds <u>clearing away</u>.
3 I'll <u>clear out</u> this desk for you, and you can put your things in it.
4 We waited for the weather to <u>clear up</u> before we resumed our march.
5 You've got no right to hunt on my land, so <u>clear off</u>.
6 Who is going to <u>clear up</u> this rubbish?
7 We still have this point to <u>clear up</u> before we can go on to consider the next one.
8 Having finished eating our lunch, we <u>cleared away</u> the dishes.

# COME

| | |
|---|---|
| **come about**<br>*vi* | happen; arise<br>*ser; ocurrir* |

Their quarrel *came about* through a slight misunderstanding.
How *does* it *come about* that he has lost three jobs in as many months?

| | |
|---|---|
| **come across**<br>*vt insep* | meet or find by chance<br>*encontrar; dar con* |

I *came across* an old school friend while on holiday in France.
Where *did* you *come across* this necklace?

| | |
|---|---|
| **come at**<br>1 *vt insep* | reach; arrive at (see 'get at' (2))<br>*averiguar; determinar* |

The truth is often difficult *to come at*.
The purpose of this investigation is *to come at* the true facts of the case.

| | |
|---|---|
| **come at**<br>2 *vt insep* | attack; assault<br>*atacar; precipitarse sobre* |

The man *came at* me with a big knife.

| | |
|---|---|
| **come back**<br>*vi* | return<br>*volver; regresar* |

Her husband went away and never *came back*.
I'*ll come back* as soon as I can manage it.

| | |
|---|---|
| **come by**<br>*vt insep* | obtain<br>*conseguir; lograr* |

How *did* you *come by* these foreign coins?
Jobs such as these are not easy *to come by* these days.

| | |
|---|---|
| **come down**<br>1 *vi* | fall; become cheaper<br>*bajar* |

The price of bread is expected *to come down* soon.
The cost of living is always going up; it never *comes down*.

| | |
|---|---|
| **come down**<br>2 *vi* | lower oneself<br>*rebajarse; humillarse* |

She *has come down* to asking for money.
I never thought he *would come down* to begging for work.

| | |
|---|---|
| **come down on**<br>*vt insep* | scold; punish<br>*echarle una bronca a uno; castigar* |

The headmaster *came down on* me like a ton of bricks.
The government intends *to come down* heavily *on* draft*
dodgers.

| | |
|---|---|
| **come in**<br>1 *vi* | enter<br>*entrar* |

I knocked on the door and was asked *to come in*.
*Come in*, please!

| | |
|---|---|
| **come in**<br>2 *vi* | become fashionable<br>*ponerse de moda* |

Mini skirts *are coming in* again after having been out of
fashion for some years.
Long hair first *came in*, in the early sixties.

| | |
|---|---|
| **come in**<br>3 *vi* | gain power; be elected (see *get in* (2))<br>*ser elegido; llegar al poder* |

*Had* the Socialists *come in* they would probably have
taken tougher measures against inflation.
When the Labour government *came in*, the country was
already in a difficult financial situation.

| | |
|---|---|
| **come into**<br>*vt insep* | inherit<br>*heredar* |

He *came into* a large sum of money when his uncle died.
She has deserted most of her old acquaintances* since
she *came into* a fortune.

| | |
|---|---|
| **come off**<br>1 *vi* | become detached<br>*desprenderse; separarse* |

Two of the buttons on my new shirt *have come off*.
The handle *came off* when she lifted the tea-pot.

| | |
|---|---|
| **come off**<br>2 *vi* | take place<br>*tener lugar* |

When does the wedding *come off*?
Her proposed visit to France never *came off*.
Steve's birthday party *came off* very well indeed.

| | |
|---|---|
| **come off**<br>3 *vi* | be successful<br>*tener éxito* |
| | His attempt to persuade the manager to give him a pay rise *did* not *come off*. |
| **come on**<br>1 *vi* | progress; develop<br>*hacer progresos; avanzar; desenvolverse* |
| | How's Freddy *coming on* in his new job?<br>The roses *are coming on* well. |
| **come on**<br>2 *vi* | begin; arrive<br>*empezar; llegar* |
| | Winter *came on* rather late this year.<br>The rain *came on* quite unexpectedly, and we were all drenched*.<br>We managed to reach the village before darkness *came on*. |
| **come on**<br>3 *vi* | (*imper.*) hurry up<br>*(imperativo) ¡vamos!; ¡date prisa!* |
| | *Come on*, girls! We are going to be late for the party.<br>Oh, *do come on*! |
| **come out**<br>1 *vi* | blossom<br>*florecer* |
| | The garden grew more and more colourful as the flowers *were coming out*.<br>When *do* the buds *come out*? |
| **come out**<br>2 *vi* | appear; become visible<br>*salir; aparecer* |
| | He likes to watch the stars *come out* at night.<br>The sun *came out* in the early afternoon. |
| **come out**<br>3 *vi* | be published (see *bring out* (2))<br>*publicarse; salir a luz* |
| | His new book *will come out* in about two weeks' time.<br>This fashion magazine *comes out* every fortnight. |

38

| | |
|---|---|
| **come out**<br>4 *vi* | be revealed; become known<br>*revelarse* |

The truth about his criminal past eventually *came out*.
Their secret is bound *to come out* sooner or later.
When it *came out* that he had been involved in the scandal, he resigned his office*.

| | |
|---|---|
| **come out**<br>5 *vi* | (of stains etc.) disappear<br>*(de una mancha, etc) quitarse* |

I twice washed the table-cloth, but the stains *would* not *come out*.

| | |
|---|---|
| **come out**<br>**with**<br>*vi insep* | say; utter<br>*soltar; salir con* |

Every time I ask him about something, he *comes out with* some funny answers.
She *came out with* a long story to explain why she did not turn up for work.

| | |
|---|---|
| **come over**<br>*vt insep* | seize; take possession of<br>*apoderarse de; atenazar; pasar* |

Panic* *came over* the passengers of the sinking ship.
What *has come over* you that you behave so irrationally?

| | |
|---|---|
| **come round**<br>1 *vi* | visit casually<br>*venir a ver; hacer una visita a* |

You can *come round* any time you like. We'll always be delighted to see you.
Why *don't* you *come round* for a drink this evening?

| | |
|---|---|
| **come round**<br>2 *vi* | regain consciousness<br>*volver en sí* |

If she *doesn't come round* soon I'm going to call for an ambulance.
How long was the old lady unconscious before she *came round*?

| | |
|---|---|
| **come round**<br>**to**<br>  *vt insep* | adopt; accept<br>*dejarse persuadir; reconocer; convencerse* |
| | One day you'*ll come round to* my way of thinking.<br>He *came round to* our point of view when he realized we were right. |
| **come through**<br>  *vi, vt insep* | survive; recover from<br>*sobrevivir; reponerse (de una enfermedad)* |
| | The explorers\* *came through* many ordeals.<br>I'm glad to hear that Arthur *has come through* (his illness). |
| **come to**<br>1  *vi* | = COME ROUND (2) |
| **come to**<br>2  *vt insep* | amount to; total<br>*sumar; hacer un total de* |
| | The money he spends on clothes *comes to* £50 a month.<br>I didn't think the electricity bill *would come to* so much. |
| **come under**<br>  *vt insep* | be classified under<br>*estar comprendido en* |
| | Books on animals *come under* 'zoology'\* in this catalogue.<br>What heading *does* this article *come under*? |
| **come up**<br>1 *vi* | arise; present itself<br>*presentarse; surgir* |
| | I haven't been able to find a job yet, but I hope something *will come up* soon. |
| **come up**<br>2 *vi* | be presented for discussion<br>*presentarse (un tema en el órden del día)* |
| | The question of finance keeps *coming up* at every meeting of the board. |
| **come up to**<br>  *vt insep* | equal; match<br>*satisfacer; llegar a un debido nivel* |
| | The results *did not come up to* our expectations.<br>His work *doesn't come up to* the required standard. |

40

**come up with**
*vt insep*

offer; produce

*proponer; sugerir*

> He *came up with* some good suggestions to improve working conditions at the factory.
> I don't suppose Edward *will come up with* any sparkling* ideas, do you?

*EXERCISE 12*

**A** Fill in the blank spaces with the correct prepositions or particles:

1 When I slammed the door, the handle came . . . in my hand.
2 The fog was gradually disappearing, and the sun was coming . . . .
3 I came . . . your cousin in the Tube* yesterday.
4 Many problems have come . . . in the course of the discussions.
5 The whole truth came . . . at the trial.
6 The sergeant came . . . . . . the soldier who was caught napping*.
7 He came . . . . . . the shocking news that Angela had committed suicide*.
8 We have come . . . worse crises* than this one.
9 The money she spends on food alone comes . . . £25 a week.
10 Have you ever come . . . the word 'ornithology'*?

**B** Answer the following questions, using phrasal verbs with *come*:

1 How did he spend the money he *inherited* under his father's will?
2 When does the price of fruit usually *drop*?
3 Did the film you saw the other day *match* your expectations?
4 How did the accident *happen*?
5 How is the new-born baby *progressing*?
6 Do you remember when the bikini first *became fashionable*?
7 Which political party *gained power* at the last general election*?
8 In which month do daffodils* normally *blossom*?
9 When did you *return* from your holiday abroad?
10 How did he *obtain* all this money?

# CUT

**cut away**
*vt sep*

remove by cutting

*cortar; separar cortando*

> The gardener *cut away* the old branches from the trees.
> The surgeon* *cut away* the diseased tissue* with infinite* precision.

41

**cut back**
1 *vt sep*

reduce
*reducir*

Owing to a sharp slump* in business, the management decided *to cut back* production by 15%.

**cut back**
2 *vt sep*

prune; cut
*podar; pelar*

The gardener *cuts* the hedge *back* two or three times a year.
Those rose-bushes ought *to be cut back* more often.

**cut down**
1 *vt sep*

fell (a tree etc.)
*talar (un árbol)*

It would be a great pity if these trees were *to be cut down*.

**cut down**
2 *vt sep*

curtail; reduce
*reducir; aminorar*

The doctor advised his patient *to cut down* smoking.
If prices continue to go up at this rate, we'll have *to cut down* our expenses.

**cut down on**
*vt insep*

consume less of
*consumir menos*

You must *cut down on* rich* food if you want to lose weight.
During the energy crisis, a lot of factories had *to cut down on* fuel.

**cut in**
*vi*

interrupt
*interrumpir*

Will you please stop *cutting in* while I'm talking!
*Don't cut in* so rudely – let him finish what he wants to say.

**cut off**
1 *vt sep*

sever
*cortar; amputar*

They have threatened *to cut off* the heads of the hostages* if the ransom is not paid promptly.
Be careful that you *don't cut* your fingers *off*!

| | |
|---|---|
| **cut off** | isolate |
| 2 *vt sep* | *aislar; bloquear; sitiar* |

A whole regiment* *was cut off* by the enemy and was forced to surrender*.
The villagers *were cut off* by the floods for nearly two weeks.

| | |
|---|---|
| **cut off** | disconnect |
| 3 *vt sep* | *cortar; desconectar* |

The Company *has cut off* our gas supply.
He was very annoyed when he *was cut off* in the middle of his phone call.

| | |
|---|---|
| **cut out** | extract or shape by cutting |
| 1 *vt sep* | *recortar; cortar* |

She *cut out* some pictures from the magazine and pinned them to the wall.
The tailor *cut out* a suit from the roll of cloth.

| | |
|---|---|
| **cut out** | stop; cease |
| 2 *vt sep* | *dejar (de hacer)* |

Why *don't* you *cut out* all this nonsense* and listen to me for a change?
I'm sick and tired of your moaning*. Just *cut* it *out*, will you?

| | |
|---|---|
| **cut out** | (*usu. pass.*) be suited for |
| 3 *vt sep* | *tener talento para; ser propio para* |

That young lady *is cut out* to be a teacher.
I really don't think I'm *cut out* for this sort of work.
William and Elizabeth seem *to be cut out* for each other.

| | |
|---|---|
| **cut out** | leave out; omit |
| 4 *vt sep* | *tachar; suprimir* |

If you intend to have your book published you will have *to cut out* all the rude words.

43

| | |
|---|---|
| **cut out**<br>5 *vt sep* | stop; refrain from<br>*dejar de (fumar, beber, etc)* |

Though his health was rapidly deteriorating* he could not *cut out* drinking.

| | |
|---|---|
| **cut up**<br>1 *vt sep* | cut into pieces<br>*cortaren pedazos; dividir* |

The butcher *cut up* the cow he had slaughtered.
The mother *cut* the cake *up* and gave the children a piece each.

| | |
|---|---|
| **cut up**<br>2 *vt sep* | distress; upset<br>*afligir; causar pena* |

The news of her husband's death *cut* her *up* quite badly.
I *was* very *cut up* when I learned that Jennifer had broken her leg.

| | |
|---|---|
| **cut up**<br>3 *vt sep* | criticise; attack<br>*criticar; atacar* |

His latest book *has been* mercilessly *cut up* by the reviewers*.

## *EXERCISE 13*

Use synonyms in place of the underlined phrasal verbs:

1 They will cut off our electricity supply if we don't pay the bill.
2 The seamstress* cut out a dress and started sewing it.
3 It is very impolite to cut in while others are speaking.
4 She cut the meat up with a sharp knife.
5 However hard he tried he could not cut out smoking.
6 We are using too much electricity; we shall have to cut down on it.
7 I feel completely cut off from the outside world.
8 She was very cut up at the news of her friend's death.
9 I can't see him as a lawyer; he doesn't seem to be cut out for that profession.
10 This article is far too long; you should cut out one or two paragraphs.

# DO

**do away with**  abolish; get rid of
1 *vt insep*  *abolir; derogar; anular*

Most countries in Europe *have done away with* capital punishment.
It's about time these old-fashioned customs *were done away with*.

**do away with**  kill; murder
2 *vt insep*  *asesinar*

The criminals *did away with* the witness who gave evidence* against them.

**do by**  treat
*vt insep*  *tratar*

A good boss is one who always *does* well *by* his employees.
Do as you *would be done by.* (proverb)

**do down**  disparage; speak ill of
1 *vt sep*  *hablar mal de; denigrar*

He'*s* always *doing* his colleagues *down* in public.

**do down**  cheat; get the better of
2 *vt sep*  *estafar; engañar*

The salesman *did* her *down* over the price of her coat.
He's the kind of man who *would do* his own mother *down*.

**do for**  help, usu. with housework
1 *vt insep*  *llevar la casa a*

Mrs. Smith *has been doing for* him since his wife died.

**do for**  (*usu. pass.*) ruin; finish off
2 *vt insep*  *(normalmente en voz pasiva) acabar con*

The country *was done for* after the earthquakes*.
The old man had been ailing for some time, but it was pneumonia that finally *did for* him.

| | |
|---|---|
| **do in**<br>1 *vt sep* | kill; murder<br>*asesinar* |
| | You'd better keep an eye on this prisoner, or he'*ll do* somebody *in* one of these days. .<br>She is not the first girl *to be done in* by this murderer. |
| **do in**<br>2 *vt sep* | (*pass.*) tired; exhausted<br>*(voz pasiva) agotado; exhausto* |
| | What's the matter, Tim? You look completely *done in.*<br>The housewife felt *done in* after the morning's work. |
| **do out**<br>*vt sep* | clean or clear out<br>*arreglar; poner en orden; limpiar* |
| | While you *do out* the cellar, I'll tidy up the living-room.<br>That cupboard *has not been done out* for months. |
| **do out of**<br>*vt sep\** | cheat (sb.) out of<br>*estafar; hacer perder (algo) por engaño* |
| | He took advantage of her naivety\* and *did* her *out of* a large sum of money.<br>The shopkeeper *did* me *out of* 50 pence. |
| **do up**<br>1 *vt sep* | renovate; modernize<br>*renovar* |
| | The landlord *did up* all the rooms in the house before letting them out.<br>How much do you think it is going to cost us *to do up* the bathroom? |
| **do up**<br>2 *vt sep* | fasten; button<br>*atar; abrochar* |
| | Hang on a minute while I *do up* my shoelaces.<br>Could you *do* my dress *up* at the back, please? |
| **do up**<br>3 *vt sep* | make into a parcel<br>*envolver* |
| | The girl at the counter *will do up* the books for you.<br>The presents *were done up* in lovely green paper. |

| | |
|---|---|
| **do with**<br>1 *vt insep* | (with 'can' or 'could') need<br>*(con CAN o COULD) venir bien* |
| | He said he could *do with* a new pair of shoes.<br>Your shirt can *do with* a good wash. It looks absolutely filthy.<br>We could *do with* a new vacuum* cleaner in this place. |
| **do with**<br>2 *vt insep* | be content with<br>*contentarse con; estar satisfecho* |
| | Until we find a better place to live in we shall have *to do with* this small flat. |
| **do with**<br>3 *vt insep* | be related to; be connected with<br>*tener que ver con; tener relación con* |
| | I don't know exactly what sort of job he has, but it is *to do with* computers*.<br>She's very interested in anything *to do with* Roman art. |
| **do with**<br>4 *vt insep* | (with *have*) have dealings with; be involved in<br>*(con HAVE) estar metido/implicado en; tener que ver con* |
| | I have nothing whatever *to do with* these men.<br>We have reason to believe that he has something *to do with* the bank raid. |
| **do without**<br>*vt insep* | manage without<br>*pasarse sin; prescindir de* |
| | Children can't *do without* the help of their parents.<br>Surely the country can *do without* fanatics* like you. |

*EXERCISE 14*

Fill in the blank spaces with the correct prepositions or particles:

1 I could do ... a nice long holiday.
2 Every summer he and his wife do ... their house.
3 The government is planning to do ...... some outdated* laws.
4 He is thinking of selling his car, but he's not sure if he'll be able to do ... it.
5 She does ... the Pearsons three mornings a week.
6 What you've just said has nothing to do ... the subject under discussion.

7 She spent all the morning doing ... the attic*.
8 She did ...... her husband by poisoning his food.
9 He was a blackmailer who deserved to be done ....
10 His employer did him ... ... his holiday pay.

# DRAW

| | |
|---|---|
| **draw in**<br>1 *vi* | (of days) become shorter<br>*(de los días) hacerse mas cortos; acortarse* |

The days *are drawing in* as autumn approaches.

| | |
|---|---|
| **draw in**<br>2 *vt sep* | involve<br>*mezclar; envolver (en un asunto)* |

She strongly objected to their evil plans and would not let herself *be drawn in.*

| | |
|---|---|
| **draw in**<br>3 *vt sep* | attract<br>*atraer* |

The new play *is drawing in* large audiences every night.

| | |
|---|---|
| **draw on**<br>*vi* | approach; come closer<br>*acercarse* |

As the date of the examination *drew on*, the candidates* grew more and more tense.
As winter *drew on*, they started preparing themselves for the cold months ahead.

| | |
|---|---|
| **draw out**<br>1 *vi* | (of days) become longer<br>*(de los días) alargarse; hacerse más largos* |

The days *are drawing out* as spring approaches.

| | |
|---|---|
| **draw out**<br>2 *vt sep** | get sb to talk<br>*hacer hablar* |

We tried to be friendly with the girl, but she was too shy *to be drawn out.*
He's that quiet type of person who needs *to be drawn out.*

| | | |
|---|---|---|
| **draw out** | prolong | |
| 3 *vt sep* | *estirar; prolongar* | |

This debate* *has been drawn out* long enough.
You *have drawn out* your essay too much. Next time try to make it brief.

| | |
|---|---|
| **draw up** | come to a halt; stop |
| 1 *vi* | *pararse* |

The bus *drew up* at the zebra* crossing.
The car *drew up* when the traffic lights changed to red.

| | |
|---|---|
| **draw up** | prepare; draft |
| 2 *vt sep* | *redactar; preparar* |

She instructed her lawyer *to draw up* a new will.
The contract *was drawn up* in the presence of two witnesses.

| | |
|---|---|
| **draw up** | set in line |
| 3 *vt sep* | *formar (tropas)* |

The officer *drew up* his men before the parade started.
The soldiers *were drawn up*, ready for inspection.


## *EXERCISE 15*

Fill in the blank spaces with the correct particles:

1 The days begin to draw ... after 21st December.
2 She has a gift of drawing ... even the most reserved* of people.
3 The taxi drew ... outside the hotel.
4 He refused to be drawn ... when the quarrel started.
5 The solicitor promised to draw ... the agreement in a day or two.
6 The days begin to draw ... after 21st June.

# FALL

**fall apart**
*vi*

disintegrate; fall to pieces
*hacerse pedazos; hundirse*

The house *is* practically *falling apart* and badly needs renovating*.
His whole life *has fallen apart* since his wife divorced* him.

**fall back**
*vi*

retreat; withdraw
*replegarse; retirarse*

As the enemy troops advanced we *fell back*.
The defeated army *fell back* in utter disarray*.

**fall back on**
*vt insep*

have recourse to
*recurrir a; valerse de; apoyarse en*

It's always good to have a friend *to fall back on*.
If the worst comes to the worst we can *fall back on* mother to lend us the money.

**fall behind**
*vi, vt insep*

slacken in pace or progress
*quedarse atrás; rezagarse*

Several of the runners *fell behind* in the Marathon*.
Lazy students invariably *fall behind* the others (in their work).

**fall behind with**
*vi*

be late in/with
*estar atrasado; tener atrasos*

He *fell behind with* his instalments* on the car.
She *has fallen behind with* the payments on the washing-machine.

**fall down**
*vi*

fall to the ground
*caerse*

She *fell down* the stairs and broke her arm.
Jack *fell down* from the tree he was climbing.

| | |
|---|---|
| **fall for**<br>1 *vt insep* | fall in love with<br>*enamorarse de*<br><br>I *fell for* that girl the first time we met.<br>She *has fallen for* that young man in a big way. |
| **fall for**<br>2 *vt insep* | be deceived by<br>*dejarse engañar por; dejarse embaucar por*<br><br>I never thought you *would fall for* that old trick.<br>Every girl seems *to fall for* his smooth talk. |
| **fall in**<br>1 *vi* | collapse; give way<br>*caer; desplomarse; venirse abajo*<br><br>The roof of the old tunnel could *fall in* any time.<br>The walls of the house *have fallen in*. |
| **fall in**<br>2 *vi* | get into line<br>*alinearse; formarse*<br><br>The sergeant ordered the soldiers *to fall in*.<br>*Fall in!* |
| **fall in with**<br>1 *vt insep* | meet by chance<br>*encontrarse con; juntarse con*<br><br>In their journey through the desert they *fell in with* a party of nomads*. |
| **fall in with**<br>2 *vt insep* | agree to; concur with<br>*convenir en; aprobar*<br><br>He says he is quite willing *to fall in with* the scheme.<br>They have finally *fallen in with* our proposals. |
| **fall off**<br>1 *vi* | diminish; dwindle<br>*disminuir; enfriarse (la amistad)*<br><br>Our exports *have fallen off* appreciably* this year.<br>'Love cools, friendship *falls off*, brothers divide.'<br>Shakespeare, *King Lear*. |

**fall off**
2 *vi*

deteriorate; worsen
*empeorar*

The service at that hotel *has fallen off* since it came under new management.

**fall out**
1 *vi*

happen; occur
*resultar*

Everything *fell out* just as we had anticipated\*.
It *fell out* that nobody was in the house the night she was murdered.

**fall out**
2 *vi*

quarrel; disagree
*pelearse*

She *has fallen out* with her sister over some trivial\* matter.
When thieves fall out honest men get their own. (proverb)

**fall out**
3 *vi*

opp. fall in (2)
*romper filas*

**fall through**
*vi*

miscarry; fail
*fracasar*

Their plans for starting a language school *fell through* for lack of capital.
No one supported the scheme and it *fell through*.

**fall to**
*vt insep*

start; begin
*empezar a; ponerse a*

No sooner had they got home than they *fell to* bickering\*.
He *fell to* wondering what to do with himself.

**fall under**
*vt insep*

be classified under
*clasificarse bajo; estar incluido en*

Which heading *does* this item\* *fall under*?
It *falls under* (the heading of) 'petty\* cash'.

| **fall (up) on** | attack; assault |
| *vt insep* | *caer sobre; atacar* |

The bandits* *fell on* the convoy* at sunset.
Enemy troops *fell upon* us from all directions.


## EXERCISE 16

Fill in the blank spaces with the correct prepositions or particles:

1 The quality of the goods we now receive has fallen .... It is not what it used to be.
2 I'm afraid I can't manage the meeting tonight, but I'll fall ...... whatever decisions you take.
3 As fresh fruit was not available we had to fall ...... tinned* fruit.
4 I'm sorry to hear that Anthony and Edward have fallen ... They were such good friends.
5 She fell ... from the roof and broke her neck.
6 He fell ... that girl as soon as he saw her.
7 Attendance at these classes has fallen ... since the new teacher took over.
8 He fell ... with the rent when he was out of work.
9 We fell ...... some interesting people from Mexico while on holiday in Spain.
10 It fell ... that I was passing by when I heard the woman screaming.
11 The project* to build a new sports centre has fallen ... for lack of adequate* funds.
12 The old shed fell ... during last night's gale.


# GET

| **get about** | move about; travel |
| 1 *vi* | *salir; viajar; moverse* |

Since he broke his leg he is finding it hard to *get about*.
Nowadays people *get about* much more than they used to.

| | |
|---|---|
| **get about**<br>2 *vi* | spread; become known<br>*saberse; divulgarse* |
| | It *got about* that she was having an affair* with the post-man.<br>The news *got about* that he was emigrating to Canada.<br>A rumour* *got about* that the wedding had been can-celled. |
| **get across**<br>*vt sep** | convey; communicate<br>*hacer entender; comunicar* |
| | He may be a very competent scientist, but he's certainly poor at *getting* his stuff *across* (to the class).<br>The speaker was trying hard *to get* his point *across* (to his audience). |
| **get ahead**<br>*vi* | pass beyond; progress<br>*(a) adelantarse a; (b) hacer progresos, avanzar* |
| | Francis *got ahead* of the runners in the race.<br>I'm pleased to hear that we *are getting ahead* with the project after all. |
| **get along**<br>1 *vi* | go; depart<br>*irse* |
| | We'd better be *getting along* before it starts raining.<br>Well, I must be *getting along* now. It's nearly one o'clock. |
| **get along**<br>**(with)**<br>2 *vi* | progress<br>*hacer progresos; avanzar; desenvolverse* |
| | How *are* you *getting along* with your French lessons?<br>We *are getting along* well with the job. |
| **get along**<br>3 *vi* | manage<br>*arreglárselas; ir tirando* |
| | I don't know how you expect me *to get along* without money.<br>You shouldn't worry too much about us. We'*ll get along* somehow. |

54

| | |
|---|---|
| **get along**<br>4 *vi* | be on good terms (with)<br>*llevarse bien con uno* |

Judith and her room-mate do not seem *to get along* well together.
It's very easy *to get along* with the new boss; he's a most charming man.

| | |
|---|---|
| **get at**<br>1 *vt insep* | reach<br>*alcanzar* |

She placed the books on the top shelf where the children could not *get at* them.

| | |
|---|---|
| **get at**<br>2 *vt insep* | find out; ascertain (see *come at* (1))<br>*descubrir; averiguar* |

The truth about his sudden resignation* was difficult *to get at.*
Our object in this inquiry is *to get at* the real causes of the crash.

| | |
|---|---|
| **get at**<br>3 *vt insep* | imply; suggest<br>*querer decir; insinuar* |

What exactly *are* you *getting at*?
I didn't quite understand what he *was getting at* by that remark.

| | |
|---|---|
| **get at**<br>4 *vt insep* | find fault with; criticize<br>*criticar; tomarla con alguien* |

For one reason or another, the teacher seems *to be* constantly *getting at* Alex.
Who *are* you *getting at* now?

| | |
|---|---|
| **get away**<br>*vi* | escape; abscond with<br>*escaparse; evadirse* |

The prisoner managed *to get away* (from his guards).
The thieves *got away* with a lot of cash and jewellery.
The cashier *got away* with all the money in the safe.

| | |
|---|---|
| **get away**<br>**with**<br>   *vt insep* | escape punishment<br>*quedar sin castigo* |
| | You really think you can *get away with* telling such obvious lies, don't you?<br>Some people can *get away with* murder. |
| **get back**<br>1 *vi* | return<br>*volver* |
| | When *did* you *get back* from your holiday in Spain?<br>I expect her *to get back* by Friday at the latest. |
| **get back**<br>2 *vt sep* | recover; regain<br>*recobrar; recuperar* |
| | Sandra never *got back* the purse she lost.<br>If you lend him your pen, you'*ll* never *get* it *back*. I know him only too well. |
| **get back at**<br>   *vt insep* | retaliate; avenge oneself<br>*desquitarse con uno; vengarse* |
| | He made a laughing* stock of me that night, but I'*ll get back at* him for this.<br>She refused to work any overtime, so the manager *got back at* her by not giving her a pay rise. |
| **get down**<br>1 *vt sep* | make a note of; record<br>*apuntar; poner por escrito* |
| | I want you *to get* his statement *down* in writing.<br>*Have* you *got* it all *down*, Mrs Briggs, or shall I repeat it for you? |
| **get down**<br>2 *vt sep** | depress<br>*deprimir; desanimar* |
| | The bad news *is getting* me *down*.<br>You mustn't let this thing *get* you *down*. Just try to forget about it. |
| **get down to**<br>   *vt insep* | apply oneself to<br>*empezar; ponerse a* |
| | I really must *get down to* some serious work this term.<br>Let's *get down to* it then, shall we? |

| **get in**<br>1 *vi* | arrive home<br>*llegar a casa* |
|---|---|

It was nearly midnight when they *got in*.
What time do you expect her *to get in*?

| **get in**<br>2 *vi* | be elected; gain power (see *come in* (3))<br>*ser elegido; llegar al poder* |
|---|---|

The Tories* *got in* with quite a big majority.
This political party *will* definitely *get in*, at the next general election.

| **get in(to)**<br>*vi, vt insep* | enter (a certain place)<br>*entrar (en un sitio)* |
|---|---|

As all the doors and windows were shut, the dog could not *get in*.
We could not *get into* the house as it was locked and we had no key with us.

| **get into**<br>*vt insep* | be involved in<br>*meterse (en dificultades); contraer (deudas)* |
|---|---|

They'*ll* soon *get into* debt if they are not careful with their spending.
Those boys *are* always *getting into* mischief.
I'm afraid he *got into* trouble with the police.

| **get off**<br>1 *vi, vt insep* | alight (from a vehicle etc.)<br>*apearse; bajar (de un autobús, etc)* |
|---|---|

Could you please tell me where *to get off*?
You *get off* at the next station.
You must never attempt *to get off* the bus while it is still in motion.

| **get off**<br>2 *vi* | escape punishment<br>*escaparse (de un castigo)* |
|---|---|

Next time you *won't get off* with just a warning; you'll probably end up in prison.
He was very lucky to *get off* with only a small fine*.

| **get on**<br>1 *vi, vt insep* | opp. get off (1).<br>*subir (a un autobús, etc)* |
|---|---|

| | |
|---|---|
| **get on**<br>2 *vi* | = get along (2), (3), (4) |

| | |
|---|---|
| **get on**<br>3 *vi* | grow old<br>*envejecer; hacerse viejo.* |

I see he's *getting on*. Sixty next month, I believe.

| | |
|---|---|
| **get on for**<br>*vt insep* | approach; draw near to<br>*andar cerca de (un edad); faltar poco para (una hora)* |

Old Mrs Williams must *be getting on for* seventy.
It *was getting on for* twelve when we reached the village.

| | |
|---|---|
| **get out**<br>1 *vi* | leave; go<br>*salir; irse* |

When he refused *to get out*, she threatened to call the police.
*Get out*, the lot of you!

| | |
|---|---|
| **get out**<br>2 *vi* | leak (of a secret); become known<br>*hacerse público; saberse* |

The news *has got out* that they were secretly engaged.
Their secret is bound *to get out* sooner or later.

| | |
|---|---|
| **get out of**<br>1 *vt insep* | escape from<br>*escaparse; evadirse* |

The rabbit *got out of* its cage because I had left the shutter open.
The convict* *has got out of* gaol by climbing a nine-foot wall.

| | |
|---|---|
| **get out of**<br>2 *vt insep* | avoid; shirk<br>*faltar a (un deber); zafarse de* |

The boy tried *to get out of* going to school by feigning* illness.
No one should be allowed *to get out of* paying his share of the bill.
You just can't *get out of* paying your debts.

| | |
|---|---|
| **get over**<br>1 *vt insep* | overcome; surmount<br>*sobreponerse a; dominar* |

The girl used to be afraid of going to the dentist\*, but she *has got over* that now.
He doesn't seem *to have got over* the shock of losing his wife.
We have quite a lot of problems *to be got over*.

| | |
|---|---|
| **get over**<br>2 *vt insep* | recover from<br>*reponerse de* |

As a little boy, Geoffrey could not *get over* the loss of his parents.
It took Lisa a few weeks *to get over* her illness.

| | |
|---|---|
| **get over**<br>3 *vt sep*\* | get finished with<br>*terminar* |

The sooner we *get* the cleaning *over* the better.
There's no point in postponing the meeting any further; we might as well *get* it *over* and done with.

| | |
|---|---|
| **get round**<br>1 *vt insep* | cajole; wheedle<br>*persuadir; engatusar a uno* |

The little girl *got round* her mother to buy her a new dress.
I'm banking\* on you, Janet, to *get round* big daddy to lend us the money.

| | |
|---|---|
| **get round**<br>2 *vt insep* | dodge; evade; circumvent<br>*pasar por alto (un problema); evitar; evadir* |

At the moment I see no way of *getting round* this problem.
It's no use trying *to get round* paying your taxes.
There're always ways and means of *getting round* the law.

| | |
|---|---|
| **get round to**<br>*vt insep* | find time to do sth.<br>*tener tiempo para* |

I always wanted to clear out the cellar, but *have* never *got round to* it.
When I finally *got round to* buying tickets for the show they were all sold out.

59

| | |
|---|---|
| **get through**<br>1 *vt insep* | complete; finish<br>*terminar; acabar* |

I'm afraid I can't lend you the book now. I *haven't got through* it yet.
Will you be able *to get through* this pile of letters by tomorrow morning?

| | |
|---|---|
| **get through**<br>2 *vi, vt insep* | pass; be successful in<br>*aprobar; tener éxito* |

The exam was quite tough, but I *got through* alright.
*Did* he *get through* his driving test this time?

| | |
|---|---|
| **get through**<br>3 *vi* | make a telephone connection<br>*comunicar con (por teléfono)* |

I couldn't *get through* (to him). The line was engaged all the time.

| | |
|---|---|
| **get through**<br>4 *vt insep* | use up; exhaust<br>*gastar; consumir* |

He'*ll* soon *get through* his savings if he goes on spending so recklessly.
The widow *got through* her late husband's money in just over a year.

| | |
|---|---|
| **get up**<br>1 *vi, vt sep\** | rise from bed; awaken<br>*levantarse* |

During the summer holidays, I used *to get up* very late.
What time *did* you *get up* this morning?
Tell the maid *to get* me *up* at seven sharp\*.

| | |
|---|---|
| **get up**<br>2 *vi* | stand up<br>*levantarse; ponerse de pie* |

The pupils *got up* when the teacher came into the classroom.
As he *was getting up* to deliver his speech, the crowd began to boo him.

60

| **get up** | organize; arrange |
| 3 *vt sep* | *organizar; preparar* |

We're *getting up* a party for Diana's birthday, so I hope you'll all be able to come.

| **get up** | dress |
| 4 *vt sep\** | *disfrazarse de; vestir; llevar* |

He *got* himself *up* as a clown for the fancy-dress\* ball.
The young ladies *were got up* in their best clothes.

## EXERCISE 17

**A** Replace the underlined words with phrasal verbs containing 'get'. In some examples more than one answer is possible:

1 How is Henry progressing in his new job?
2 I wish I could finish all this work by tomorrow.
3 It took her a long time to recover from the death of her only child.
4 The teacher did not seem to be able to communicate the new material to his students.
5 The Society has organized a nation-wide campaign\* to raise funds for the disabled\*.
6 The bank robbers escaped with fifty thousand pounds.
7 He rises from bed at six every morning.
8 This kind of thing really depresses me.
9 She can't reach the top shelf without a ladder.
10 She left her handbag in the train, but recovered it from the Lost Property Office.

**B** Fill in the blank spaces with the correct prepositions or particles. In some examples more than one answer is possible:

1 Unless Oliver works very hard he won't get ... his final exams.
2 She never quite got ... the shock of being deserted by her husband.
3 Thanks to his diligence\*, Gilbert got ... of the rest of the class.
4 How are you getting ... with your thesis\*?
5 Let's get the washing-up ... before we go to the cinema.
6 A car stopped in front of the house, and a smartly dressed lady got ... .
7 Work and worry are getting me ... .
8 I'd better be off now; it must be getting ... ... ten o'clock.
9 I always wanted to paint the windows, but have never got ... ... it.
10 You shouldn't let him get ... ... a mean trick like that.

61

# GIVE

**give away**
1 *vt sep*

give free of charge
*regalar*

He *gave away* his entire fortune to charitable foundations*.
My aunt *has given* her old clothes *away* (to the poor).

**give away**
2 *vt sep*

distribute; present
*distribuir; entregar*

A member of the royal family *gave away* the trophies.
At the end of each year the headmaster *gives away* the certificates to the students.

**give away**
3 *vt sep*

betray; divulge; reveal
*traicionar; revelar*

The spy* said he would rather die than *give away* his country.
He said that he was not a foreigner, but his accent *gave* him *away*.

**give back**
*vt sep*

return
*devolver*

Having finished reading the book I *gave* it *back* (to the library).

**give in**
1 *vi*

surrender; yield
*rendirse; ceder*

The besieged* army was forced *to give in* when it ran out of ammunition*.
He says he is not going *to give in* to blackmail*, no matter what happens.

**give in**
2 *vt sep*

submit; tender
*presentar; entregar*

Candidates who wish to take this exam should *give in* their applications* not later than September 20th.
She was not satisfied with her job and decided *to give in* her notice.

| | |
|---|---|
| **give off**<br>  *vt insep* | emit; produce<br>*emitir; producir* |
| | Oil refineries *give off* a lot of fumes*.<br>Burning rubber *gives off* an unpleasant smell. |
| **give on to**<br>  *vt insep* | overlook; provide access to<br>*dar a* |
| | Their house *gives on to* the sea.<br>The back door *gives on to* the garden. |
| **give out**<br>1 *vi* | come to an end; become exhausted<br>*agotarse; acabarse* |
| | Our food supplies were about *to give out* when the search party found us.<br>My patience is beginning *to give out*. |
| **give out**<br>2 *vi* | cease to function<br>*averiarse; fallar* |
| | For no apparent reason, the car engine suddenly *gave out*. |
| **give out**<br>3 *vt sep* | distribute<br>*repartir; distribuir* |
| | A boy standing in the street *gave out* leaflets* to people passing by.<br>The invigilators* *gave out* the exam papers to the students. |
| **give out**<br>4 *vt sep* | announce; make known<br>*anunciar; divulgar* |
| | The newscaster *gave out* the news of the air disaster*<br>in a grave voice.<br>It *was given out* that the enemy had suffered heavy casualties* from the air-raid*. |
| **give out**<br>5 *vt insep* | = give off |

| | |
|---|---|
| **give up**<br>1 *vi* | despair; admit defeat<br>*perder la esperanza; desesperar; rendirse* |
| | We mustn't *give up* yet; we may still find them.<br>I can't work out this problem; I *give up*. |
| **give up**<br>2 *vt insep* | stop; abandon<br>*dejar de (fumar, beber, etc)* |
| | The old man *did not give up* horse-riding until he was sixty.<br>I tried *to give up* smoking, but without success.<br>He gave up the study of Greek long ago. |
| **give up**<br>3 *vt sep* | surrender; part with<br>*entregar(se); rendirse; ceder* |
| | The fugitive* could not stand being on the run for so long and decided *to give* himself *up* (to the police).<br>He *gave up* his seat on the train to an elderly man.<br>The President refused *to give up* the documents on grounds of national security. |
| **give up**<br>4 *vt insep* | relinquish<br>*abandonar; dimitir de (un puesto)* |
| | They *have given up* the idea of emigrating to Canada.<br>She had *to give up* her job when she got married. |
| **give up**<br>5 *vt sep* | devote<br>*dedicar* |
| | The teachers *gave up* the last hour of their meeting to discussing the problem of truancy*.<br>The priest's life *was given up* to the worship* of God. |

*EXERCISE 18*

Use synonyms in place of the underlined phrasal verbs:

1 I pleaded* with him to let the boy come with us, but he refused to give in.
2 She gave back all the money she had borrowed from me.
3 Just as we were about to reach our destination the petrol gave out.
4 You must give up eating sweets if you want to get slim.

5 The news of the president's assassination* was <u>given out</u> on the radio shortly before midnight.
6 This electric fire doesn't <u>give out</u> a lot of heat.
7 He <u>gave away</u> all his money to a charity*.
8 Steam engines <u>give off</u> a lot of smoke.
9 One of us here must have <u>given away</u> the secret.
10 He seems determined not to <u>give up</u> his claim to the property.
11 Their villa <u>gives on to</u> the river.
12 They have <u>given up</u> all hope of finding any survivors of the air crash.
13 When did you <u>give in</u> your essay?
14 Oh, you do <u>give up</u> too easily, don't you?
15 The minister himself <u>gave away</u> the prizes.

# GO

| | |
|---|---|
| **go about**<br>1 *vi* | move from place to place<br>*andar (de un sitio a otro); circular* |

These men always *go about* in gangs.

| | |
|---|---|
| **go about**<br>2 *vi* | circulate<br>*circular; correr (rumores, etc)* |

A rumour *is going about* that Simon and Julie are getting engaged.
The story *is going about* that they are leaving town for good.

| | |
|---|---|
| **go about**<br>3 *vt insep* | approach; tackle<br>*tratar; enfocar* |

The matter is extremely delicate. We'll have *to go about* it carefully.
How do you propose *to go about* this problem?

| | |
|---|---|
| **go about with**<br>*vt insep* | keep company with<br>*salir con uno; salir juntos* |

He *is going about with* a most beautiful girl.
Derek and Patricia *have been going about* (*with* each other) for some time now.

| **go after** | pursue; try to catch |
| 1 *vt insep* | *seguir; perseguir* |

The farmer *went after* the fox with a shotgun.
The police *went after* the escaped prisoner and tracked*
him down a few miles from the village.

| **go after** | try to get |
| 2 *vt insep* | *andar tras uno (o algo)* |

These two young men *are going after* the same girl.
He's *going after* the first prize. I know he wouldn't settle
for less than that.

| **go against** | oppose; be contrary to |
| 1 *vt insep* | *oponerse a; ir en contra de* |

She *went against* her parents' wishes in refusing to marry
that man.
This kind of thing *goes against* my principles.

| **go against** | be unfavourable to |
| 2 *vt insep* | *ser desfavorable a; ir mal a* |

Luck *went against* our team in the end and we lost the
game.
They realized only too late that the war *was going against*
them.

| **go ahead** | proceed; continue |
| 1 *vi* | *seguir (adelante); continuar* |

'May I use your telephone?' 'Please *go ahead*'.
We have decided not *to go ahead* with the project, after
all.

| **go ahead** | make progress |
| 2 *vi* | *avanzar; hacer progresos* |

The project seems *to be going ahead* well.
Once the dispute was settled, production in the plant
*went ahead* full steam.

**go along**
*vi*

proceed (with a certain activity)
*avanzar; seguir*

You will learn more about the work as you *go along*.

**go along with**
1 *vt insep.*

accompany
*acompañar*

He *went along with* his guests as far as the station.
Would you like me *to go along with* you to the doctor, or would you rather go alone?

**go along with**
2 *vt insep*

agree with; co-operate with
*estar de acuerdo con*

I'm afraid I can't *go along with* you on that point.
I *go along with* you all the way.
We are quite willing *to go along with* you in this scheme.

**go around**
*vi*

= go about (1), (2)

**go at**
1 *vt insep*

attack; assault
*lanzarse sobre; atacar*

The crazed man *went at* me with a knife.

**go at**
2 *vt insep*

set about energetically
*emprender; lanzarse sobre*

Once he decided to do the job, he *went at* it for all he was worth.

**go away**
*vi*

go; depart; leave
*irse; marcharse*

I wish you *would go away* and leave me in peace.
*Are* you *going away* for Christmas*, or are you staying at home?

**go back**
1 *vi*

return
*volver; regresar*

When do you intend *to go back* (to your country)?
He *went back* to the office to collect the papers he had left behind.

| | |
|---|---|
| **go back**<br>2 *vi* | revert<br>*volver a; volver sobre* |

Let's leave this point for the moment. We'*ll go back* to it later.
But *to go back* to the problem of rising unemployment. . . . What's the government going to do about it?

| | |
|---|---|
| **go back**<br>3 *vi* | date back (to)<br>*remontarse hasta* |

Their family *goes back to* the Norman Conquest.
This custom *goes back to* the Elizabethan times.

| | |
|---|---|
| **go back on**<br>*vt insep* | fail to keep (one's word, promise, etc.)<br>*faltar a; desdecirse de (lo prometido)* |

They *have gone back on* their promise to lend us the money.
An honest man never *goes back on* his word.

| | |
|---|---|
| **go beyond**<br>*vt insep* | exceed; surpass<br>*exceder; ir mas allá de* |

His account of what had happened *went beyond* credibility.
The good results *went beyond* our wildest dreams.

| | |
|---|---|
| **go by**<br>1 *vi* | pass by<br>*pasar delante (de)* |

The parade *went by* amid a warm applause* from the watching crowd.

| | |
|---|---|
| **go by**<br>2 *vi* | elapse<br>*pasar; transcurrir* |

We were growing impatient as time *went by* and nothing happened.
As the months *went by* he got accustomed to the daily routine of prison life.

| | |
|---|---|
| **go by**<br>3 *vt insep* | be guided by<br>*decidir; juzgar (según las apariencias)* |

One cannot always *go by* appearances, can one?
We have very little evidence *to go by*.

| | |
|---|---|
| **go down**<br>1 *vi* | sink<br>*hundirse* |
| | The ship *went down* on her maiden\* voyage to Australia.<br>The small boat sprang a leak\* and *went down* within seconds. |
| **go down**<br>2 *vi* | (of the sun etc.) set<br>*(del sol) ponerse* |
| | In the summer months the sun *goes down* very late. |
| **go down**<br>3 *vi* | fall; drop<br>*bajar* |
| | The price of fruit usually *goes down* in summer.<br>The patient's temperature *went down* to 36.8 degrees. |
| **go down**<br>4 *vi* | be received (well/badly)<br>*gustar a uno (mucho/poco); ser recibido; caer (bien o mal)* |
| | His made-up story *went down* well with his friends.<br>The director's speech *went down* very badly at last night's dinner. |
| **go for**<br>1 *vt insep* | attack<br>*atacar; acometer* |
| | The dog *went for* the intruder\* and chased him out of the building.<br>The wounded bull *went for* the matador\*. |
| **go for**<br>2 *vt insep* | go to fetch or get<br>*ir por; ir a buscar a* |
| | You look very ill, Morris. Shall I *go for* the doctor?<br>I am *going for* a drink. Will you join me? |
| **go for**<br>3 *vt insep* | apply to; be true of<br>*referirse a; ser aplicable a; ir por* |
| | What I have said about William *goes for* the rest of you, too.<br>I want everybody to leave this room, and that also *goes for* you, Barbara. |

| | |
|---|---|
| **go in for**<br>1 *vt insep* | participate in; enter for<br>*inscribirse; presentarse; participar* |

Amanda is *going in for* a beauty contest\*.
Are you *going in for* the 1000 metres race?

| | |
|---|---|
| **go in for**<br>2 *vt insep* | adopt as a hobby or occupation<br>*dedicarse a* |

She *goes in for* swimming and tennis.
When he left college he *went in for* teaching.

| | |
|---|---|
| **go into**<br>*vt insep* | investigate; consider; discuss<br>*(a) examinar; investigar; (b) discutir* |

The detective promised that he *would go into* my case at once.
These proposals *will have to be gone into* very carefully before a final decision can be taken.
We *are* not *going into* that again, are we?

| | |
|---|---|
| **go off**<br>1 *vi* | leave (a certain place)<br>*irse; marcharse* |

She *went off* to visit her mother abroad.
He *has gone off* to Greece for a short holiday.

| | |
|---|---|
| **go off**<br>2 *vi* | be fired; explode<br>*dispararse; estallar* |

The gun *went off* accidentally, and wounded him in the thigh.
The boy was seriously injured when a firework\* *went off* in his face.

| | |
|---|---|
| **go off**<br>3 *vi* | go bad; deteriorate<br>*pasarse; deteriorarse* |

The meat you bought the other day *has gone off*.
Don't eat that steak. It'*s going off*.
Her work *has gone off* very much lately.

70

| | |
|---|---|
| **go off**<br>4 *vi* | take place in a specified manner.<br>*resultar; salir* |
| | Everything *went off* without a hitch\*.<br>How *did* the interview *go off*?<br>The party *went off* very badly this time. |
| **go off**<br>5 *vi* | fall asleep<br>*dormirse* |
| | He *went off* by the fire while he was watching television. |
| **go on**<br>1 *vi* | continue; last<br>*durar; continuar* |
| | I wonder how much longer this cold weather *will go on*!<br>It looks as though this war *will go on* forever. |
| **go on**<br>2 *vi* | happen; take place<br>*pasar; ocurrir* |
| | There is something fishy\* *going on* in that place.<br>What the hell *is going on* here? |
| **go on about**<br>*vt insep* | = keep on about |
| **go out**<br>1 *vi* | leave the house (implies a leisure activity)<br>*salir (de la casa)* |
| | The weather is lovely; why don't we *go out* for a walk?<br>They don't *go out* much these days. |
| **go out**<br>2 *vi* | cease to be fashionable; become obsolete<br>*pasar de moda; caer en desuso* |
| | Mini-skirts *went out* a few years ago.<br>This method of printing is gradually *going out*. |
| **go out**<br>3 *vi* | be extinguished<br>*apagarse* |
| | During the thunderstorm all the lights in the house *went out*.<br>The fire *went out* as I forgot to poke\* it. |

| | |
|---|---|
| **go over**<br>1 *vt insep* | examine; review; inspect<br>*examinar; revisar; inspeccionar* |

The auditor\* *went over* the accounts carefully.
Let's *go over* the details of the plan once more.
We *went over* the house for almost two hours and decided not to buy it.

| | |
|---|---|
| **go over**<br>2 *vt insep* | search<br>*revisar; examinar* |

The customs\* officer *went over* my luggage, item\* by item.
The police officer *went over* the suspect\* very thoroughly, but did not find any hidden weapons.

| | |
|---|---|
| **go round**<br>*vi, vt insep* | be sufficient (for all).<br>*alcanzar para todos; ser suficiente* |

Don't you worry, dear! There is enough food *to go round*.
Twenty bottles of wine *will not go round* so many guests.

| | |
|---|---|
| **go through**<br>1 *vt insep* | = go over (1), (2) |

| | |
|---|---|
| **go through**<br>2 *vt insep* | suffer; endure; experience<br>*sufrir; pasar por* |

She *has gone through* a lot with her first husband.
They *have gone through* a terrible ordeal.
The country *is going through* a critical period.

| | |
|---|---|
| **go through**<br>3 *vt insep* | use up; consume<br>*gastar (dinero); consumir* |

He *has* already *gone through* the money he inherited from his uncle.
You would wonder how much food this little boy *could go through*.

| | |
|---|---|
| **go through**<br>**with**<br>*vt insep* | complete; bring to a finish<br>*llevar a cabo* |

I realize it is not going to be such a profitable deal, but all the same we must *go through with* it.
He says that he can't *go through with* the marriage.

| **go under** | = go down (1) |
| *vi* | |

| **go up** | increase; rise |
| 1 *vi* | *subir* |

The price of beef *has gone up* a lot since last October.
It was announced that the fees* for the next academic
year *would go up* by £200.

| **go up** | explode |
| 2 *vi* | *estallar; estallar en llamas* |

The bridge *went up* with a deafening bang.
The helicopter crashed and *went up* in flames.

| **go with** | suit; match |
| *vt insep* | *hacer juego; ir con* |

You look ridiculous in that hat. Can't you see it *doesn't*
*go with* your dress?
These colours *go* nicely *with* each other.

| **go without** | forgo; do without |
| *vt insep* | *pasarse sin algo* |

We can't *go without* sleep for much longer.
It looks as though we shall have *to go without* a holiday
this summer.
If you can't afford to buy a new suit now, you'll just have
*to go without*.

## *EXERCISE 19*

**A** Fill in the blank spaces with the correct prepositions or particles. In
some examples more than one answer is possible:

1 He went . . . . . . this exam last year, but failed it.
2 The party went . . . until after midnight.
3 If there is not enough coffee to go . . . someone will have to go . . . .
4 Prices always seem to be going . . . . They never go . . . .
5 The bomb went . . . before the police could defuse it.
6 Do you go . . . . . . stamp-collecting?
7 I have no intention of going . . . . . . my word.
8 He wants to get a residence permit, but he does not know how to
go . . . it.

73

9 I don't want you to help me, so please go . . . .
10 We'll soon go ... our coal supply if we don't start economizing.

**B**  Use synonyms in place of the underlined phrasal verbs:

1 I'll explain the new vocabulary* as we <u>go along</u>.
2 The milk has <u>gone off</u> because she forgot to put it in the fridge.
3 The price of petrol will <u>go up</u> by 2p a gallon as from January.
4 He <u>went on</u> working till three in the morning.
5 Almost two years have <u>gone by</u> since we last saw him.
6 She loves to watch the sun <u>go down</u>.
7 I wonder why they <u>went off</u> in such a hurry!
8 We <u>went through</u> his papers carefully, but found nothing suspicious.
9 You <u>go back</u> now and we will come later.
10 Your brother is not very fond of work, and that <u>goes for</u> you too.
11 That yellow tie doesn't <u>go with</u> your shirt.
12 Don't <u>go by</u> what Charles says; he knows nothing about farming.
13 Bob thinks Italy will win. Do you <u>go along</u> with that?
14 The lamp in the bathroom suddenly <u>went out</u>.
15 Two fishing-boats <u>went down</u> in the storm.

# HAND

| | |
|---|---|
| **hand back**<br>*vt sep* | return; give back<br>*devolver* |

Please remember *to hand back* the cassettes you've borrowed from me. I need them for tomorrow.

| | |
|---|---|
| **hand down**<br>*vt sep* | (*usu. pass.*) transmit; bequeath<br>*pasar; transmitirse* |

These customs *have been handed down* from generation to generation.
We didn't exactly buy this antique furniture. It *was handed down* to us by great-grandfather.

| | |
|---|---|
| **hand in**<br>*vt sep* | submit; tender<br>*presentar; entregar* |

The minister *handed in* his letter of resignation to the cabinet.
I would advise you *to hand in* your application as early as possible.

74

| **hand on** | = hand down |
|---|---|
| *vt sep* | |

| **hand out** | distribute; give out |
|---|---|
| *vt sep* | *distribuir; repartir* |

There was a young woman in the street, *handing out* leaflets to passers-by.

| **hand over** | deliver; surrender |
|---|---|
| *vt sep* | *entregar* |

The Brazilian police refused *to hand over* the fugitive to the British authorities*.
The retiring premier* *will hand over* charge of his office on January 18th.

*EXERCISE 20*

Fill in the blank spaces with the correct particles:

1 As soon as I've finished marking your papers I'll hand them ... to you.
2 This legend* has been handed ... from father to son.
3 Over a thousand copies of the sales brochure* have now been handed ....
4 When the customs officer asked to see my passport I handed it ... to him.
5 She handed ... her notice yesterday and is leaving at the end of the month.

# HANG

| **hang about** | loiter (near a place) |
|---|---|
| 1 *vi, vt insep* | *esperar (en un lugar); rondar* |

We spent almost an hour just *hanging about*, waiting for you to come.
Did you notice any suspicious-looking men *hanging about* the building at the time of the robbery?

| **hang about** | = hang on (1), hold on (1) |
|---|---|
| 2 *vi* | |

**hang around**
*vi, vt insep*
= hang about (1)

**hang back**
*vi*
hesitate; show reluctance to act
*vacilar; dudar*

He *hung back* when they asked for blood-donors*.
I suspected there was something fishy about the business, and *hung back* from taking part in it.

**hang on**
1 *vi*
Wait; *(see hold on (1))*
*esperar*

Just *hang on* a second while I do up my dress.
Don't worry if you can't make it at seven sharp. I'*ll hang on* until eight o'clock.

**hang on**
2 *vt insep*
depend on
*depender de; estar pendiente de*

Everything *hangs on* what happens next.
His whole political career *hangs on* the result of tomorrow's election.

**hang on to**
*vt insep*
keep; retain possession of
*agarrarse a; guardar*

I'd *hang on to* that oil painting if I were you. It might be worth a lot more in a year or two.
We must *hang on to* whatever we have.

**hang together**
1 *vi*
support one another
*mantenerse unidos; apoyarse*

We can overcome these difficulties if we *hang together*.
Old friends must *hang together* at all times.

**hang together**
2 *vi*
be consistent
*corresponder; coincidir*

Their statements do not seem *to hang together* at all.
His story doesn't quite *hang together*, does it?

76

| **hang up** | end a telephone call abruptly |
| 1 *vi, vt insep* | *colgar (el teléfono)* |

She didn't give me a chance to explain; she just *hung up* (on me).

| **hang up** | delay; hinder |
| 2 *vt sep* | *detener; parar* |

We *were hung up* for nearly thirty minutes during the thick fog.
I'm sorry to arrive so late, but I *got hung up* in a traffic* jam.

*EXERCISE 21*

Fill in the blank spaces with the correct prepositions or particles:

1 The trouble with John is that he can never hang . . . . . . his jobs for very long.
2 Those two men have been hanging . . . the place all morning. I wonder what they are up to!
3 If you'll hang . . . a minute, sir, I'll go and check our files.
4 It all hangs . . . now. I can see why they left in such a hurry.
5 No one hung . . . when we asked for volunteers*.
6 Work on the railway track has been hung . . . for several weeks because of the heavy snow.
7 It all hangs . . . whether he is willing to back our claim.
8 The family hung . . . well during that crisis.

# HOLD

| **hold back** | control; restrain |
| 1 *vt sep* | *contener; retener; reprimir (lágrimas)* |

The police could do nothing *to hold back* the angry crowds.
She was so upset about it that she could not *hold back* her tears.

| | |
|---|---|
| **hold back**<br>2 *vt sep* | withhold; delay<br>*retener (un pago); no revelar; mantener en secreto* |
| | This information will have *to be held back* from the witnesses until after the trial.<br>There will be angry protests from the transport workers if their wage increases *are held back* for much longer. |
| **hold down**<br>1 *vt sep* | keep at a low level<br>*limitar; restringir* |
| | The government came in for sharp criticism from the Opposition\* leader for failing *to hold down* prices.<br>Unless our expenditure\* *is held down*, we'll soon go bankrupt\*. |
| **hold down**<br>2 *vt sep* | suppress; oppress<br>*oprimir; agobiar* |
| | The country *is* being ruthlessly\* *held down* by the occupying armies. |
| **hold forth**<br>*vi* | harangue; make a speech<br>*arengar; hablar largamente; disertar sobre* |
| | He *held forth* at great length on the evils of the permissive\* society. |
| **hold in**<br>*vt sep* | suppress; restrain<br>*contener; dominar* |
| | You must learn *to hold in* your bad temper.<br>She's used to *holding in* her feelings. |
| **hold off**<br>1 *vi* | (of rain etc.) stay away<br>*(a) no llover; (b) mantenerse a distancia* |
| | I hope the rain will *hold off* until after the match. |
| **hold off**<br>2 *vt sep* | keep at a distance<br>*rechazar; defenderse de* |
| | The besieged garrison\* *held off* enemy attacks for several days. |

78

| | |
|---|---|
| **hold on**<br>1 *vi* | wait (see *hang on* (1))<br>*esperar* |
| | If you *hold on* a moment, madam, I'll go and see if Mr Jones is free.<br>Just *hold on* a second while I put my shoes on. |
| **hold on**<br>2 *vi* | see *hold out* (2) |
| **hold on to**<br>*vt insep* | keep in one's hands or possession<br>*agarrarse a; guardar* |
| | He mananged *to hold on to* the rope until he was rescued.<br>He wanted to sell that piece of land, but I persuaded him *to hold on to* it. |
| **hold out**<br>1 *vi* | last; continue<br>*durar* |
| | Our food supplies won't *hold out* for much longer.<br>How long *will* these provisions* *hold out*? |
| **hold out**<br>2 *vi* | continue to resist<br>*resistir; defenderse* |
| | The small force *held out* heroically against overwhelming odds.<br>The beleaguered* town *held out* for four weeks till re-inforcements* arrived. |
| **hold over**<br>*vt sep** | (*usu. pass.*) postpone; defer<br>*(normalmente en voz pasiva) aplazar(se)* |
| | The last item* on the agenda* *will be held over* until the next meeting.<br>The decision to close down the factory *has been held over* until April. |
| **hold to**<br>*vt insep* | adhere to<br>*atenerse a; cumplir* |
| | I think we ought to *hold to* our original plan.<br>He *has* never *held to* his principles very firmly. |

| | |
|---|---|
| **hold together**<br>*vi, vt sep* | remain or keep united<br>*mantener(se) unido(s)* |

We can only hope that the country *will hold together* during this crisis.
If he can't *hold* the Party *together*, no one can.

| | |
|---|---|
| **hold up**<br>1 *vt sep* | delay; hinder<br>*detener; retrasar* |

We *were held up* in a traffic jam for nearly one hour.
Mail delivery *has been held up* for a few days as a result of the post office workers' strike.

| | |
|---|---|
| **hold up**<br>2 *vt sep* | stop with intent to rob<br>*asaltar; atracar* |

The police are reported to be looking for three men who *held up* a mail van in East London this morning.
Two armed men *held up* the bank in broad daylight.

| | |
|---|---|
| **hold with**<br>*vt insep* | approve of; agree with<br>*aprobar; estar de acuerdo con* |

They don't *hold with* Communism and all that it stands for.
Do you *hold with* smoking in cinemas?

## EXERCISE 22

Fill in the blank spaces with the correct prepositions or particles:

1 I simply couldn't hold ... my anger. The whole thing was outrageous*.
2 The Catholic Church does not hold ... divorce.
3 The train was held ... by fog for almost two hours.
4 Lazy, restless people can't hold ...... their jobs.
5 Hold ... a minute! Can't you see I'm busy?
6 I don't hold ... all this talk about women's* lib and sex* equality.
7 They were held ... at gun point by three masked men.
8 The garrison held ... for two weeks before surrendering.
9 Does he still hold ... what he said last time?
10 The family has always held ... in difficult times like these.
11 If you want me to help you, then don't try to hold the truth ... from me.
12 We have been held ... by this dictator long enough; it's time we got rid of him.

# KEEP

**keep at**
*vt insep*

persist in; persevere in
*perseverar en; persistir en*

Arthur *kept at* his German until it was perfect.
You will never finish the job unless you *keep at* it.

**keep away**
*vi, vt sep\**

(cause to) stay away
*(a) evitar contacto con; mantenerse a distancia; (b) no dejar a uno tocar; mantener a distancia*

He *kept away* from his friends for several months.
You'd better *keep away* from that girl, or you'll get yourself into trouble.
*Keep* the child *away* from that fire.

**keep back**
1 *vi, vt sep*

(cause to) stay back
*no dejar avanzar; no avanzar; mantenerse a distancia*

The firemen asked the crowd *to keep back* from the burning building.
*Keep back*, or I'll shoot!
The policemen could do nothing *to keep* the jubilant\* fans *back* from the pitch.

**keep back**
2 *vt sep*

conceal; keep secret
*ocultar; no revelar*

We were certain she *was keeping* something *back* from us, but we didn't know exactly what.
For the time being, all the names of the witnesses will have *to be kept back*.

**keep back**
3 *vt sep*

hinder; impede; delay
*estorbar; impedir; retrasar*

What *has kept* you *back* for so long?
I hope I'm not *keeping* you *back* from your work.

**keep down**
1 *vt sep\**

repress; hold in subjection
*oprimir*

The conquered peoples *were kept down* by cruel, restrictive laws.

| | |
|---|---|
| **keep down**<br>2 *vt sep* | keep low<br>*mantener bajo; controlar* |

The government seems unable *to keep down* prices. They are going up all the time.
Ask those two men *to keep* their voices *down*. I can hardly hear a word of what the speaker is saying.

| | |
|---|---|
| **keep from**<br>*vt insep* | avoid; refrain from<br>*abstenerse de; guardarse de* |

You should *keep from* making promises you know you can't fulfil.
Though his health was rapidly deteriorating, he could not *keep from* alcohol.

| | |
|---|---|
| **keep in**<br>1 *vt sep* | detain after school hours as a punishment<br>*hacer quedarse en la escuela (como castigo)* |

The schoolmaster *kept in* all the pupils who had not done their homework.

| | |
|---|---|
| **keep in**<br>2 *vt sep* | restrain; suppress<br>*contener; refrenar* |

She is very good at *keeping in* her emotions.
The speaker managed *to keep* his indignation* *in*, in spite of the provocative* remarks from the audience.

| | |
|---|---|
| **keep in with**<br>*vt insep* | remain friendly with<br>*mantener buenas relaciones con* |

You should *keep in with* your boss if you expect any further promotion.
When she won a fortune on the pools* all her friends and relatives tried *to keep in with* her.

| | |
|---|---|
| **keep off**<br>1 *vi* | (of rain, etc.) stay away<br>*(a) no llover; (b) mantenerse a distancia* |

Fortunately, the rain *kept off* the whole afternoon and we were able to finish our game.

| | |
|---|---|
| **keep off**<br>2 *vi, vt sep* | (cause to) stay at a distance from<br>*(a) no dejar a uno tocar algo; (b) no pisar (la hierba); no tocar* |
| | '*Keep off* the grass!' (sign displayed in public parks).<br>This barbed* wire is meant *to keep* trespassers* *off*. |
| **keep on**<br>*vi* | (followed by gerund) continue<br>*seguir (haciendo); insistir en* |
| | Don't *keep on* telling me what to do; I'm perfectly capable of making my own decisions.<br>Why do you have *to keep on* bothering me? |
| **keep on<br>about**<br>*vt insep* | keep talking about (sb. or sth.) (see *go on about*)<br>*estar todo el tiempo hablando de* |
| | The way she *keeps on about* her son! It's enough to bore anyone to tears.<br>I wish that woman wouldn't *keep on about* her arthritis*; I'm sick and tired of listening to her. |
| **keep on at**<br>*vt insep* | pester with requests, etc.<br>*seguir pidiendo; molestar a uno pidiendo* |
| | He won't give you back your money unless you *keep on at* him all the time. |
| **keep out**<br>*vi, vt sep* | (cause to) stay outside<br>*no permitir entrar/pasar* |
| | 'Private. *Keep out!*' (notice on door)<br>Tell those kids *to keep out* of my study*, please!<br>These old windows *do* not *keep out* the draught*.<br>You really mustn't *keep* the cat *out* in this cold weather. |
| **keep out of**<br>*vt insep* | not interfere in<br>*no meterse en* |
| | Now you *keep out of* this! It's no concern of yours.<br>I'd *keep out of* their quarrel if I were you. |
| **keep to**<br>*vt insep* | adhere to<br>*atenerse a; cumplir; mantener (promesas)* |
| | He's not the kind of person who *keeps to* his promises.<br>Please make sure that this schedule *is* strictly *kept to*. |

| | |
|---|---|
| **keep up**<br>1 *vt sep* | maintain; continue<br>*mantener; seguir* |

You are doing just fine, Sally. *Keep* it *up*!
They had *kept up* a steady correspondence for nearly eight years.
We should try *to keep up* these old customs of our ancestors\*.

| | |
|---|---|
| **keep up**<br>2 *vt sep* | maintain in good condition<br>*mantener* |

We can no longer afford *to keep up* this big house, so we may have to sell it and buy a smaller one.

| | |
|---|---|
| **keep up**<br>3 *vt sep*\* | delay from going to bed<br>*tener despierto; hacer trasnochar* |

The baby was sick last night and *kept* us *up* until the small hours.
We'd better be off now; we don't want *to keep* you *up*.

| | |
|---|---|
| **keep up with**<br>*vt insep* | keep pace with<br>*mantenerse a la altura de* |

Can Russia *keep up with* America in the field of space technology?
Eva has to work very hard in order to *keep up with* her classmates.


*EXERCISE 23*

Fill in the blank spaces with the correct prepositions or particles:

1 They are finding it difficult to keep ... such a large house.
2 Tell that man to keep his cattle ... my land.
3 She keeps ... ... her ailments\* for hours on end.
4 Don't walk so fast; I can't keep ... ... you.
5 Her mother kept her ... from school yesterday to help her with some housework.
6 Don't keep ... interrupting him; let him finish what he has to say.
7 She kept ... ... her husband until he agreed to buy her a new washing-machine.
8 They kept the bad news ... from her for as long as they could.
9 This new anorak I've bought you should keep ... the cold.

10 You will soon finish this work if you keep ... it for a few more days.
11 We have been kept ... in our training programme by shortage of qualified staff.
12 The shopkeeper has kept ... his reputation* by selling first-class goods.
13 You should keep ... doing anything that might antagonize* him.
14 The teacher kept Elizabeth ... yesterday for being late.
15 The rebellious* tribes could only be kept ... by cruel measures.

# KNOCK

**knock about**
1 *vt insep*

wander here and there
*recorrer; vagar por*

Our son *has knocked about* the world a great deal.
He *has been knocking about* Africa ever since he left the army.

**knock about**
2 *vt sep**

treat roughly; maltreat
*pegar; maltratar; golpear*

It's wrong *to knock* your children *about* in this way.
The furniture *has been* badly *knocked about*.

**knock back**
1 *vt sep*

drink at one gulp
*beber de un trago*

He ordered a pint of beer and *knocked* it *back* in ten seconds.
She *knocked back* two double brandies.

**knock back**
2 *vt sep**

= set back (3)

**knock down**
1 *vt sep*

strike to the ground
*(a) derribar; (b) atropellar*

The boxer *knocked down* his opponent with a single punch.
The old man *was knocked down* by a lorry as he was crossing the street.

85

| | |
|---|---|
| **knock down**<br>2 *vt sep* | demolish; pull down<br>*derribar; demoler* |

Quite a lot of old houses in this area *have been knocked down* and replaced by modern blocks of flats.

| | |
|---|---|
| **knock down**<br>3 *vt sep* | sell at an auction<br>*adjudicar a uno (en una subasta)* |

The auctioneer\* *knocked* the painting *down* to an art dealer from Paris.
That beautiful mahogany\* desk *was knocked down* to me for only a fiver.

| | |
|---|---|
| **knock down**<br>4 *vt sep* | reduce (a price, etc.)<br>*rebajar* |

The shopkeeper *knocked* the price *down* from £10 to £8.

| | |
|---|---|
| **knock off**<br>1 *vi* | stop work<br>*suspender; terminar (el trabajo); dar de mano* |

We usually *knock off* at about five o'clock.
What time do you *knock off* for lunch?

| | |
|---|---|
| **knock off**<br>2 *vt sep* | cause to fall<br>*hacer caer; tirar* |

You'd better keep an eye on the child, or he'*ll knock* that vase *off*.
The unfortunate jockey\* was knocked off his horse and broke his arm.

| | |
|---|---|
| **knock off**<br>3 *vt sep* | compose hurriedly<br>*hacer rápidamente; terminar* |

I'm not surprised he got a low mark for his essay. He *knocked* it *off* in less than an hour.
She *knocked off* an article for a magazine in about two hours.

| | |
|---|---|
| **knock off**<br>4 *vt sep* | deduct<br>*rebajar (en); descontar* |

I'*ll knock off* 40p if you want to buy the book.
The shopkeeper *knocked* four pounds *off* the bill.

| | |
|---|---|
| **knock out**<br>1 *vt sep* | render unconscious<br>*(a) poner fuera de combate; dejar KO; (b) dejar sin*<br>*sentido* |

The boxing champion\* *knocked* his challenger\* *out* in the
fourth round of the fight
It only took three glasses of wine *to knock* him *out* for
the rest of the evening.

| | |
|---|---|
| **knock out**<br>2 *vt sep* | eliminate from a competition<br>*eliminar* |

Italy *knocked* England *out* (of the World Cup), and *were*
themselves *knocked out* by Holland.

| | |
|---|---|
| **knock up**<br>1 *vt sep* | rouse; awaken<br>*despertar; llamar* |

Tell the maid *to knock* me *up* at eight sharp.
People don't like being *knocked up* in the middle of the
night.

| | |
|---|---|
| **knock up**<br>2 *vt sep* | prepare quickly<br>*preparar rápidamente* |

She *knocked up* a meal for her unexpected guests.
I don't have time to cook a proper lunch, so I'*ll* just
*knock up* a snack\* for us.

| | |
|---|---|
| **knock up**<br>3 *vt sep*\* | exhaust<br>*agotar* |

I don't want you *to knock* yourself *up* like that.
What's the matter, Jim? You look quite *knocked up*.

*EXERCISE 24*

Fill in the blank spaces with the correct prepositions or particles:

1. The workmen usually knock ... for tea at three o'clock.
2. Her husband knocks her ... a bit, but she has learnt to put up with it.
3. Our team was knocked ... of the competition earlier than expected.
4. They have knocked that old house ... and built a new one in its place.
5. He has been knocking ... Scandinavia for some time, but he is now back home.
6. She was knocked ... by a taxi and had to be taken to hospital.

87

7. The salesman agreed to knock five pounds ... the price of the radio.
8. I was completely knocked ... after that long journey.
9. The boxer regained his title by knocking his opponent* ....
10. I have to get up early tomorrow, so could you please knock me ... at six?

# LAY

**lay aside**
1 *vt sep*

place to one side
*dejar; poner a un lado*

He *laid aside* his book and listened to what I had to tell him.

**lay aside**
2 *vt sep*

abandon; disregard
*dejar a un lado; olvidar*

At such a time of crisis, party differences should be *laid aside*.

**lay aside**
3 *vt sep*

save for the future (see *put aside/away/by*)
*ahorrar; poner aparte*

You should look ahead and try *to lay aside* some money for your retirement*.
We have a few hundred pounds *laid aside* for emergencies.

**lay down**
1 *vt sep*

place down
*(a) deponer (armas); (b) depositar; poner*

They *laid down* the heavy box gently.
The soldiers *laid down* their arms (i.e. surrendered).
She *laid* the baby *down* on the bed.

**lay down**
2 *vt sep*

impose; prescribe
*poner; asentar; dictar*

The bank *has laid down* certain conditions on which the loan may be granted.
He is that type of person who likes *to lay down* the law.
The rules of procedure in a conference *are laid down* to deal with any point of order.

88

| | |
|---|---|
| **lay down**<br>3 *vt insep* | (with 'life') sacrifice<br>*(con LIFE) dar; sacrificar* |

A man who *lays down* his life for his country is certainly worthy of praise.
This was a cause\* which they believed was just, and for which they were prepared *to lay down* their lives.

| | |
|---|---|
| **lay in**<br>*vt sep* | store<br>*acumular; comprar; proveerse de* |

Make sure you *lay in* plenty of food and drink for the week-end.
We *laid in* a large supply of sugar before it went up in price.

| | |
|---|---|
| **lay off**<br>1 *vt sep* | dismiss temporarily<br>*despedir (obreros)* |

The factory *has laid off* some two hundred workers during the last three months.
More and more people *are being laid off* every day as a result of the present economic depression\*.

| | |
|---|---|
| **lay off**<br>2 *vt insep* | desist from<br>*dejar de* |

If only you'd *lay off* smoking for a while, I'm sure you'd feel much better.
*Lay off* teasing that cat, Janet!

| | |
|---|---|
| **lay on**<br>1 *vt sep* | supply; provide<br>*instalar; conectar* |

How long will it take *to lay on* water in this house?
We'll move into our new cottage as soon as gas and electricity *have been laid on.*

| | |
|---|---|
| **lay on**<br>2 *vt sep* | arrange; organize<br>*organizar; preparar* |

They *have laid on* a splendid concert for their distinguished visitors.
We *are laying on* a party for Joanna's birthday.

| **lay on**<br>3 *vt sep* | apply; spread<br>*poner; pintar; echar (una capa de pintura)* |
|---|---|

There is still one more coat of paint *to be laid on.*

| **lay out**<br>1 *vt sep* | spend; disburse<br>*gastar; invertir* |
|---|---|

We had *to lay out* every penny we had saved on that house.
I *have* already *laid out* an awful lot of money on repairs to this car.

| **lay out**<br>2 *vt sep* | make unconscious<br>*(a) dejar sin sentido; derribar; (b) debilitar* |
|---|---|

He received a blow on his chin, which *laid* him *out.*
The heat of the sun *laid* her *out.*

| **lay out**<br>3 *vt sep* | plan; arrange<br>*trazar; componer; confeccionar (un libro)* |
|---|---|

The gardener *laid out* the flower-beds* very neatly.
The printer *lays out* the pages of a book.

| **lay out**<br>4 *vt sep* | prepare for burial<br>*amortajar* |
|---|---|

The undertaker* carefully *laid out* the corpse*.
The corpse *is* now *laid out* and ready for burial.

| **lay up**<br>1 *vt sep* | store; stock<br>*ahorrar; acumular* |
|---|---|

'*Lay* not *up* for yourselves treasures upon earth, where moth* and rust doth corrupt, and where thieves break through and steal: but *lay up* for yourselves treasures in heaven.' – The Bible

| **lay up**<br>2 *vt sep* | take out of service<br>*poner fuera de servicio* |
|---|---|

I've had *to lay up* my car; I simply can't afford the petrol.
These ships *have been laid up* for repairs.

90

| **lay up** | (*usu. pass.*) confine to bed |
| 3 *vt sep* | *obligar a guardar la cama* |

A really bad attack of 'flu can *lay* you *up* for days.
He *was laid up* for two months with a broken leg.

*EXERCISE 25*

Use synonyms in place of the underlined phrasal verbs:
1 Owing to the drop in sales, the factory is <u>laying</u> some of the men <u>off</u>.
2 You should try to <u>lay</u> your prejudices* <u>aside</u> and judge the case on its merits.
3 The grounds of the mansion were <u>laid out</u> by a landscape architect.
4. I wish you would <u>lay off</u> drink for a little while!
5 Electricity will be <u>laid on</u> in the house within the next few days.
6 She has been <u>laid up</u> with malaria for the last two weeks.
7 The government is <u>laying out</u> large sums of money on its development programmes.
8 He usually <u>lays up</u> his car during the winter months.
9 You just can't <u>lay down</u> hard and fast rules.
10 They <u>laid up</u> large supplies of coal for the severe winter ahead.
11 We have a nice little sum of money <u>laid aside</u> for a rainy day.
12 She <u>laid in</u> a good stock of rice in case of a shortage.

# LEAVE

| **leave aside** | disregard; not consider |
| *vt sep* | *dejar de un lado; no hacer caso de* |

I don't quite see how you can *leave aside* the fact that the man is a crook*.
Let us *leave* this matter *aside* for the moment, shall we?

| **leave behind** | fail to bring; forget to take |
| 1 *vt sep* | *olvidar; dejar* |

Next time you come to see us, remember not *to leave* Marilyn *behind.*
She *left* her luggage *behind* in the train.
I can't give you a lift today, as I have *left* the car *behind.*

| **leave behind** | outstrip |
| 2 *vt sep* | *dejar atrás* |

Towards the end of the race, Alan was rapidly *leaving* the other runners *behind*.
In mathematics, she *leaves* everyone else way *behind*.

| **leave off** | stop; cease |
| 1 *vi, vt insep* | *terminar; dejar de* |

It started to rain at six in the evening, and never *left off* all night.
Last time, we *left off* at the end of Lesson Four.
*Leave off* arguing you two, and get on with the job.

| **leave off** | cease to wear |
| 2 *vt sep* | *quitarse; no ponerse (ropa)* |

Now that the winter months are over, we can *leave off* our woolen garments.
In this cold climate, winter clothing cannot usually *be left off* before May.

| **leave on** | allow to stay in position |
| 1 *vt sep* | *dejar puesto* |

He *left on* his hat when he went into the house.
Don't remove that cover; *leave* it *on*.

| **leave on** | not switch off |
| 2 *vt sep* | *dejar encendido;dejar puesto* |

Don't *leave* the television *on* when you are not watching it.
The light in the bathroom *had been left on* all night.

| **leave out** | leave outside |
| 1 *vt sep\** | *dejar fuera* |

He went in and *left* the others *out* in the rain.
If you *leave* your toys *out* at night, darling, someone might steal them.

| | |
|---|---|
| **leave out**<br>2 *vt sep* | omit; skip<br>*omitir; olvidar; pasar por alto* |

Before we can print this book, you will have *to leave out* all the four-letter\* words.
It would be a great pity *to leave* this material *out*.
You *left out* one crucial point, didn't you?

| | |
|---|---|
| **leave out**<br>3 *vt sep* | exclude (from)<br>*excluir* |

Make sure you don't *leave out* anyone from the invitations.
He *has been left out* of the team, after all.

| | |
|---|---|
| **leave over**<br>1 *vt sep\** | postpone; defer<br>*aplazar* |

This matter will have *to be left over* until we meet again in April.

| | |
|---|---|
| **be left over**<br>2 *vt sep* | remain<br>*quedar; sobrar* |

When they had finished eating, there *was* hardly any food *left over*.


## EXERCISE 26

Fill in the blank spaces with the correct particles:

1 Tell that girl to leave ... crying, will you?
2 He left his coat ... in the office, and had to go back for it.
3 She took up the tale at the point where she had left ....
4 You can leave that light ... ; I'll switch it off when I go to bed.
5 The last item on the agenda will be left ... until our next meeting.
6 We left ... our sweaters when the weather got warm.
7 The editor could not publish my article in its entirety, so I had to leave parts of it ....
8 Please don't leave me ... ; I want to come with you.
9 We normally leave ... work at about five every day.
10 Let us leave that question ... now and concentrate on this one.

# LET

**let down**
1 *vt sep*

lower
*dejar caer; soltar*

He *let down* the rope to the men below.
When she *lets* her hair *down* it almost reaches her waist.

**let down**
2 *vt sep*

lengthen (a garment)
*alargar (un vestido)*

Your dress is too short and needs *to be let down* several inches.

**let down**
3 *vt sep*

fail; disappoint
*fallar a uno*

He never *lets down* anyone who turns to him for help.
I'll do everything I can to help you. I won't *let* you *down*.

**let in**
*vt sep*

allow to enter
*dejar entrar; hacer pasar*

She opened the door and *let* the cat *in*.
These old leather boots *let in* a lot of water.
Don't *let* any strangers *in* while we are out.

**let in for**
*vt sep\**

involve sb. in
*causar; plantear (problemas) a uno*

You realize what you have *let* yourself *in for* by signing those papers, dont't you?
He has *let* us *in for* a lot of extra work by failing to turn up.

**let off**
1 *vt sep*

excuse; punish lightly
*perdonar; no castigar*

I'*ll let* you *off* this time if you promise never to do it again.
The magistrate\* *let off* the petty\* thief with a small fine.

94

| | |
|---|---|
| **let off**<br>2 *vt sep* | explode; discharge<br>*disparar; hacer estallar* |
| | In England it is traditional that children *let off* fireworks on November 5th.<br>He *let* the gun *off* accidentally and wounded himself in the thigh. |
| **let on**<br>*vi* | tell (esp. sth. secret)<br>*revelar; decir* |
| | She knew who the culprit* was, but she did not *let on*.<br>Don't *let on* that I've given you a pay rise. I don't want the others to know about it. |
| **let out**<br>1 *vt sep* | allow to go out<br>*soltar; dejar escapar* |
| | Open the gate and *let out* the cattle!<br>Some boys *let* the air *out* of the front tyres of my car. |
| **let out**<br>2 *vt sep* | disclose; divulge<br>*revelar; divulgar* |
| | Please keep this information to yourself. Don't *let* it *out* to anyone else.<br>I should like to know who *let out* the secret. |
| **let out**<br>3 *vt sep* | make looser (a garment)<br>*ensanchar (un vestido); sacar de ancho* |
| | The dress is not a bad fit, but it needs *letting out* a little round the waist. |
| **let out**<br>4 *vt insep* | utter<br>*gritar; echar (un grito)* |
| | The injured man *let out* a cry of pain.<br>She *let out* a loud scream which was heard in the whole building. |
| **let up**<br>1 *vi* | abate; stop<br>*moderarse; parar* |
| | The storm raged all day, showing no signs of *letting up*.<br>'Has the rain *let up* yet?' 'No, it's still pouring down'. |

| | |
|---|---|
| **let up** | slacken one's efforts |
| 2 *vi* | *ir mas despacio; bajar el rendimiento* |

We can't afford *to let up*, now that we've nearly accomplished* our task.

He worked at it all day; he never *let up* for a moment.

## EXERCISE 27

Fill in the blank spaces with the correct particles:

1 Caroline has put on so much weight that she has had to let ... all her clothes.
2 We mustn't let ... about where they are hiding.
3 He was very lucky to be let ... with a warning and no other punishment.
4 If the pain doesn't let ... and he can't sleep, give him a sedative.*
5 Miraculously, no one was hurt when a bomb was let ... inside the shopping centre.
6 The news must have been let ... to the Press by some officials in this department.
7 I thought I could rely on your discretion,* but you let me ....
8 You are letting yourself ...... a lot of unnecessary trouble.
9 To lengthen a skirt is to let it ....
10 The door-keeper won't let ... anyone who hasn't got a membership card.

# LOOK

| | |
|---|---|
| **look after** | take care of |
| *vt insep* | *(a) cuidar de; guardar; (b) defender(se)* |

The nurse *looks after* the children when we go away.

I'm perfectly capable of *looking after* myself.

She obviously knows how *to look after* her body.

| | |
|---|---|
| **look at** | gaze at |
| 1 *vt insep* | *mirar* |

She stood *looking at* the painting in admiration.

The two men *looked* uneasily *at* each other.

*To look at* him you'd never think he was a professor.

| | |
|---|---|
| **look at**<br>2 *vt insep* | examine; inspect<br>*examinar; estudiar* |

The doctor *looked at* my knee and said there was nothing wrong with it.
We must *look at* the question from all sides.

| | |
|---|---|
| **look at**<br>3 *vt insep* | view; see<br>*mirar; ver* |

Being not so young, she *looks at* life differently from you and me.
Everyone has his own way of *looking at* things.

| | |
|---|---|
| **look at**<br>4 *vt insep* | (*usu. neg.*) consider<br>(*normalmente negativo*) *considerar* |

He wouldn't even *look at* my offer.
They refuse *to look at* our proposals.

| | |
|---|---|
| **look away**<br>*vi* | turn the eyes in another direction<br>*apartar la mirada* |

When he entered the room the girl was partially undressed, and they both *looked away* in embarrassment.

| | |
|---|---|
| **look back**<br>1 *vi* | look behind<br>*mirar hacia atrás* |

Don't *look back* now, but I think we are being followed.

| | |
|---|---|
| **look back**<br>2 *vi* | reflect upon the past<br>*recordar* |

*Looking back*, I suppose we are no better off than we were twenty-five years ago.
People like *to look back* on the good old days.

| | |
|---|---|
| **look down**<br>*vi* | look downwards<br>*mirar hacia abajo* |

He leaned over the window-sill* and *looked down* at the trees below.
The little girl *looked down* shyly·and would not speak to anyone.

**look down on**
*vt insep*

despise; regard with contempt
*despreciar; desdeñar*

One should never *look down on* people merely because they are poor.
These days unskilled workers are *looked down on* by everyone.

**look for**
1 *vt insep*

search for; seek
*buscar*

She *is looking for* a job as a shorthand* typist.
We *are looking for* a young man with drive* and initiative* to fill this vacancy*.
What *are* you *looking for*?

**look for**
2 *vt insep*

expect
*esperar; buscar*

I warned you not to get involved with that fellow, so don't *look for* any help from me now.
What do you *look for* in a woman?

**look forward to**
*vt insep*

anticipate with pleasure
*estar deseando; apetecerle a uno mucho*

We *are looking forward to* meeting your wife.
I *am looking forward to* the Christmas holidays.

**look in**
*vi*

pay a short visit (to)
*hacer una visita a; ir a ver*

The doctor *will look in* again this evening to see if everything is all right.
*Look in* on me next time you are in London, won't you?

**look into**
*vt insep*

investigate; examine
*investigar; examinar*

The police said that they *would look into* the matter at once.
Your complaint is being carefully *looked into*.

| | |
|---|---|
| **look on** | be a spectator |
| 1 *vi* | *observar; mirar* |
| | They stood *looking on* while he was being attacked. |
| | I don't want to take part in this game; I'd rather *look on*. |
| **look on** | consider; regard |
| 2 *vt insep* | *considerar a; juzgar* |
| | Some people *look on* him as a hero; others as a traitor\*. |
| | He *is looked (up)on* as the greatest novelist of his time. |
| **look on to** | overlook; face |
| *vt insep* | *dar a* |
| | Their house *looks on to* Hyde Park. |
| | My bedroom *looks on to* the river. |
| **look out** | look outwards |
| 1 *vi* | *mirar (hacia fuera)* |
| | She stood at the window and *looked out* at the hills. |
| **look out** | (*usu. imper.*) take care! beware! |
| 2 *vi* | (*imperativo*) ¡ Ten cuidado! ¡Ojo! |
| | *Look out*! The road is icy |
| | *Look out*! You nearly ran over that child. |
| **look out for** | watch for |
| 1 *vt insep* | (a) *esperar; buscar* (b) *tener cuidado con* |
| | *Look out* for me at the station. I'll be at the information desk. |
| | When you walk through that field you must *look out for* snakes. |
| **look out for** | search carefully for |
| 2 *vt insep* | *buscar* |
| | We've been *looking out for* a new house for the last two months, but haven't found anything suitable yet. |
| **look out on** | = look on to |
| *vt insep* | |

**look over**  inspect; examine.
*vt sep*  *revisar; examinar*

We ought to get a surveyor* *to look over* the house before we decide to buy it.
I'd like you *to look* the contract *over* for me if you can spare the time.
*Look over* your essay before you hand it in.

**look round**  = look back (1)
1 *vi*

**look round**  tour; visit (a place)
2 *vi, vt insep*  *visitar; darse una vuelta por*

We did not have much time *to look round* (the city).
A party of foreign visitors *were looking round* the factory this morning.

**look through**  direct the eyes through
1 *vt insep*  *mirar por*

She *looked through* the window at the snow-covered hills.
He *looked through* his binoculars* to get a clearer view of the castle.

**look through**  examine; study; peruse
2 *vt insep*  *(a) estudiar; examinar; (b) hojear*

*Look through* these photographs and see if you can pick her out.
He always *looks through* the morning papers before breakfast.
We *have looked through* our files*, but found no one by the name of Bloggs.

**look to**  attend to; take care of
1 *vt insep*  *ocuparse de; tener cuidado que*

Every citizen must *look to* his duties.
*Look to* it that this doesn't happen again.

100

| | |
|---|---|
| **look to**<br>2 *vt insep* | turn to; rely on<br>*contar con; acudir a* |
| | He is hardly the right person *to look to* for advice.<br>'You can always *look to* me for help', said the father to his son. |
| **look up**<br>1 *vi* | look upwards<br>*levantar los ojos; mirar hacia arriba* |
| | He lay down on the bed and *looked up* at the ceiling.<br>She didn't even *look up* from her book when I came into the room. |
| **look up**<br>2 *vi* | improve<br>*mejorar; ir mejor* |
| | If they can afford a new house things must be *looking up* for them.<br>Thank goodness the weather *is looking up*. |
| **look up**<br>3 *vt sep* | visit (a person)<br>*ir a ver; hacer una visita a* |
| | When you go to Italy, Frank, I'd like you *to look up* an old friend in Rome.<br>She always *looks* me *up* when she is in town. |
| **look up**<br>4 *vt sep* | search for; try to find<br>*buscar* |
| | You can *look up* the difficult words in your dictionary.<br>Would you be kind enough *to look up* the time of the next bus to Leeds for me? |
| **look up and<br>down**<br>*vt sep\** | look at (sb.) contemptuously<br>*mirar de arriba a abajo* |
| | The sergeant *looked* the soldier *up and down* and ordered him to button his uniform. |
| **look up to**<br>*vt insep* | admire; regard with esteem<br>*admirar; respetar* |
| | She *looks up to* people with plenty of money.<br>Teenagers\* usually *look up to* pop\* stars. |

**A** Use synonyms in place of the underlined phrasal verbs:

1 We must get a plumber to <u>look at</u> those pipes.
2 Business has been rather slack lately, but now it seems to be <u>looking up</u>.
3 I've <u>looked for</u> my lighter everywhere, but I still can't find it.
4 They wouldn't even <u>look at</u> my suggestion.
5 Will you <u>look after</u> the baby while I go shopping?
6 Two boys were having a fight while their friends were <u>looking on.</u>
7 Do <u>look</u> me <u>up</u> if ever you come to Oxford.
8 We <u>are looking into</u> the possibility of offering you a permanent contract with our firm.
9 <u>Look through</u> the agreement before you sign it.
10 I've always <u>looked on</u> you as one of my best friends.

**B** Fill in the blank spaces with the correct prepositions or particles:

1 Look . . . on your way home. I have something important to tell you.
2 If you go swimming there you must look . . . . . . sharks.
3 The police are looking . . . three men who broke out of gaol yesterday.
4 If you don't have her number with you look it . . . in the telephone directory.
5 We are looking . . . . . . seeing you again, Geoffrey.
6 Look . . . ! There is a car coming.
7 When I passed her in the street she just looked . . . pretending not to see me.
8 The old actress looked . . . wistfully* on her youth.
9 She heard a noise behind her and looked . . . to see what it was.
10 They are very snobbish* and look . . . . . . the working-class.

# MAKE

| | |
|---|---|
| **make after**<br>*vt insep* | pursue; chase<br>*seguir; perseguir* |

The policeman *made after* the thief.
The dogs *made after* the rabbit at an incredible speed.

| | |
|---|---|
| **make at**<br>*vt insep* | attack; lunge at<br>*lanzarse sobre; atacar* |

The man *made at* me with a big knife.

| | |
|---|---|
| **make away**<br>**with**<br>*vt insep* | kill; murder<br>*matar; asesinar* |
| | He *made away with* his wife by poisoning her food.<br>She threatened *to make away with* herself if he ever left her. |
| **make for**<br>1 *vt insep* | go towards; head for<br>*dirigirse a; encaminarse a* |
| | The ship *was making for* Dover.<br>Where *are* you *making for*? |
| **make for**<br>2 *vt insep* | lead to; result in<br>*conducir a; crear* |
| | Money does not always *make for* happiness.<br>Hygienic* kitchens *make for* healthy homes. |
| **make off**<br>*vi* | escape; run away<br>*largarse; escaparse* |
| | As soon as they saw the policeman coming, the thieves *made off*. |
| **make off**<br>**with**<br>*vt insep* | decamp with<br>*llevarse* |
| | The robbers *made off with* a lot of cash and jewellery.<br>Some boys *have made off with* our luggage. |
| **make out**<br>1 *vt sep* | write; complete<br>*escribir; llenar; rellenar* |
| | He *made out* a cheque for two hundred pounds.<br>*Make out* a list of the things you need at the grocer's.<br>Applications for this post should be *made out* in duplicate. |
| **make out**<br>2 *vt sep* | pretend; claim; maintain<br>*dar a entender que; dar la impresión de que* |
| | She *makes* herself *out* to be wealthier than she really is.<br>He *made out* that he had no previous knowledge of the deal.<br>He is not so bad as he *is made out* to be. |

| | |
|---|---|
| **make out**<br>3 *vt sep* | understand<br>*entender; explicarse* |

He is a strange sort of fellow. I cannot *make* him *out* at all.
I can't *make out* why she hasn't told me about it before.

| | |
|---|---|
| **make out**<br>4 *vt sep* | distinguish; discern<br>*distinguir; vislumbrar* |

I couldn't *make out* his face; it was too dark.
We could just *make* the castle *out* in the distance.

| | |
|---|---|
| **make out**<br>5 *vt sep* | decipher<br>*descifrar; leer* |

Can you *make out* the postmark on this letter?
See if you can *make out* this signature.

| | |
|---|---|
| **make over**<br>*vt sep* | transfer the ownership of sth.<br>*traspasar; ceder* |

He *has made over* his estate to his niece.
The bulk of the property *was made over* to the eldest son.

| | |
|---|---|
| **make up**<br>1 *vi, vt sep* | apply cosmetics to the face<br>*maquillarse; pintarse* |

A young girl like you shouldn't need *to make up*.
It takes my wife ages *to make up* her face.
He doesn't like women who *are* heavily *made up*.

| | |
|---|---|
| **make up**<br>2 *vt sep* | invent; fabricate<br>*inventar; fabricar* |

I'm not very good at *making up* excuses, I'm afraid.
Now admit it; you *made* that story *up*, didn't you?
I wish you would stop *making* things *up*, Janice!

| | |
|---|---|
| **make up**<br>3 *vt sep* | compensate for, recoup<br>*(a) recuperar; (b) indemnizar* |

We expect the government *to make up* our loss in profits this year.
There is a lot of leeway* *to make up* if you want to have a chance of passing your exams.

| | |
|---|---|
| **make up**<br>4 *vt sep* | complete; supplement<br>*completar; cubrir* |

How much do you need *to make up* the total?
We still need a hundred pounds *to make up* the deficit.*

| | |
|---|---|
| **make up**<br>5 *vt insep* | compose; constitute; form<br>*componer; integrar* |

Thirty-three different countries *make up* the British Commonwealth.
The human body *is made up* of millions of cells.

| | |
|---|---|
| **make up**<br>6 *vt sep* | compound; put together<br>*preparar (una receta); reunir* |

The chemist *made up* the doctor's prescription*.
She *made up* a bundle of old clothes and sent it off to a charity.

| | |
|---|---|
| **make up**<br>7 *vt sep* | tailor; sew<br>*confeccionar* |

If you take this suit length to the tailor, he'll *make* it *up* for you.
'Customers' own materials *made up*'. (notice outside tailor's shop)

| | |
|---|---|
| **make up**<br>8 *vi, vt sep* | become reconciled; settle (a quarrel)<br>*hacer las paces* |

After their quarrel they kissed and *made up*.
It's time you *made up* that silly quarrel.
Have Paul and Jean *made* it *up* yet?
Has Paul *made* it *up* with Jean yet?

| | |
|---|---|
| **make up**<br>9 *vt sep* | (with 'mind') come to a decision<br>*(con MIND) decidirse; resolver* |

Have you *made up* your mind yet?
You have a whole week in which *to make up* your mind.
My mind *is made up*. I am not going on that trip.

| | |
|---|---|
| **make up for**<br>*vt insep* | compensate for<br>*(a) recuperar (tiempo perdido); (b) indemnizar; compensar* |

You must work very hard now *to make up for* all the time you have wasted.
You had better *make up for* the damage you have caused.

| | |
|---|---|
| **make up to**<br>*vt insep* | ingratiate oneself with<br>*congraciarse con; intentar ganar la amistad de* |

The new secretary has already started *making up to* the boss.
He is tired of being constantly *made up to* by his juniors.

## EXERCISE 29

Replace the underlined words with phrasal verbs containing *make*:

1 The audience largely <u>consisted</u> of very young men and women. (*use the passive*)
2 There was so much noise that I could not <u>understand</u> what the speaker was saying.
3 I don't believe a word of what he said. I think he <u>invented</u> it all.
4 The dictator has <u>killed</u> most of his opponents.
5 His handwriting is very difficult to <u>decipher.</u>
6 The bandits <u>pursued</u> us on horseback.
7 We could just <u>discern</u> the ship on the horizon.
8 As soon as they finished work they <u>headed for</u> the local pub.
9 I haven't much money on me. Do you mind if I <u>write</u> you a cheque?
10 A year before he died grandfather <u>transferred</u> the business to me.
11 The boys <u>ran away</u> when they caught sight of me.
12 He is not so stupid as some people <u>maintain.</u>
13 Unlike children, adults don't <u>settle</u> their quarrels quickly.
14 The cashier has <u>decamped with</u> almost five hundred pounds.
15 I hope this cheque will <u>compensate for</u> all the trouble you have gone through.
16 Good working conditions <u>lead to</u> increased productivity.

106

# PASS

**pass away**
1 *vi*

die
*fallecer; morir*

The old man *passed away* peacefully in his sleep.
I'm sorry to hear that your father *has passed away.*

**pass away**
2 *vi*

disappear; vanish
*desaparecer; olvidarse; pasar*

The old cultural values seem to have *passed away.*
Let us hope our difficulties *will* soon *pass away.*

**pass by**
1 *vi, vt insep*

go past
*pasar (delante de)*

I saw her *passing by* only a short while ago.
The procession *passed by* our house.

**pass by**
2 *vt sep**

ignore, overlook
*(a) pasar por alto; (b) perdonar*

He had hoped for promotion, but they *passed* him *by*
in favour of a younger man.
I cannot *pass* this insult *by* without a protest.

**pass down**
*vt sep*

(*usu. pass.*) transmit; bequeath (see *hand down*)
*(normalmente en voz pasiva) pasar; transmitir*

These folk songs *have been passed down* from generation
to generation.
We didn't buy this silver ourselves; it *was passed down* to
us by great-grandfather.

**pass for**
*vt insep*

be accepted as; be taken for
*pasar por*

In his day he *passed for* a great pianist.
With an accent like that he could quite easily *pass for*
a German.

**pass off**
1 *vi*

disappear; end gradually
*pasar; desaparecer*

I am glad your headache *has passed off*.
The pain *will pass off* quickly when you have taken this medicine.

**pass off**
2 *vi*

take place; be completed
*resultar; salir*

We had expected a lot of trouble at that meeting, but fortunately it *passed off* very quietly.
The concert *passed off* quite smoothly.

**pass off**
3 *vt sep* *

represent falsely as.
*hacer(se) pasar por*

..He tried *to pass* himself *off* as a university lecturer.
He *passed* his companion *off* as a retired army officer.

**pass on**
1 *vi*

= pass away (1)

**pass on**
2 *vi*

move on; proceed
*pasar*

We've discussed this subject long enough; I think we should *pass on* to a different one.
Let us *pass on* to the next item on the agenda, shall we?

**pass on**
3 *vt sep*

communicate; convey
*comunicar; dar; hacer llegar a*

Please *pass* this message *on* to the rest of your friends.
The news of the king's arrival *was passed on* by word of mouth.

**pass out**
*vi*

faint; lose consciousness
*perder el conocimiento; desmayarse*

People often *pass out* in crowded places.
She nearly *passed out* when she heard the news.

**pass over**
1 *vi*

= pass away (1)

108

| | |
|---|---|
| **pass over**<br>2 *vt sep* | = pass by (2) |
| **pass up**<br>*vt sep* | let slip; miss<br>*perder; desaprovechar; dejar pasar* |

You should never have *passed up* such a good deal.
She *passed up* a marvellous opportunity to become an actress.

## EXERCISE 30

Use synonyms in place of the underlined phrasal verbs:

1 The demonstration passed off without incident.
2 He read the note and passed it on to his neighbour.
3 We waited for the funeral* procession* to pass by.
4 He speaks English well enough to pass for a native (*use the passive*).
5 She passed up a good chance to study abroad.
6 The legend has been passed down from father to son.
7 He passed away yesterday at dawn.
8 The intense heat of the sun made her pass out.
9 He tried to pass his secretary off as his wife.
10 We cannot pass over this incident without a formal protest.

# PAY

| | |
|---|---|
| **pay back**<br>1 *vt sep* | repay; pay in return<br>*pagar; reembolsar; devolver* |

She *paid back* the money she had borrowed from me.
I must *pay* Mr Jones *back* the £200 he lent me.
The loan will have *to be paid back* to the bank with 12% interest*.

| | |
|---|---|
| **pay back**<br>2 *vt sep* | retaliate; revenge oneself<br>*vengarse en uno; hacer pagar a* |

He *paid* her *back* for her infidelity* by going out with another woman.
I'll *pay* him *back* for this insult, you can be sure of that.

**pay for**
*vt insep*

be punished for
*pagar (caro/con la vida)*

He *paid for* his rashness* with his life.
They made him *pay* dearly *for* it.

**pay in(to)**
*vt sep*

deposit in an account
*ingresar (en una cuenta)*

The young couple *paid in* all their savings *to* a building*
society.
Please *pay* this sum *into* my partner's account.

**pay off**
1 *vi*

prove profitable
*tener éxito; ser provechoso; compensar*

Buying second-hand machinery never *pays off* in the long
run.
The scheme *has paid off* rather handsomely.

**pay off**
2 *vt sep*

recompense and dismiss from service
*pagar y despedir (obreros, etc)*

They *have paid off* fifty of their employees during this
month alone.
The crew of the ship *were paid off* at the end of the
voyage.

**pay off**
3 *vt sep*

settle (a debt etc.)
*liquidar; saldar; amortizar*

Have we *paid off* all our outstanding* debts yet?
It took him two full years *to pay* that loan *off.*

**pay out**
1 *vt sep*

disburse; hand out (money)
*pagar; desembolsar*

We've had *to pay out* an awful lot of money this year
on repairs to that house.
The cashier *pays* the salaries *out* at the end of each
month.

**pay out**
2 *vt sep*

= pay back (2)

**pay up**
*vi*

pay money owed in full
*pagar lo que se debe*

Unless you *pay up* we shall have to take you to court.
Since we have no other choice, we might as well *pay up*.

*EXERCISE 31*

Fill in the blank spaces with the correct prepositions or particles. In some examples more than one answer is possible:

1 Don't you think it's time you paid him . . . the money you owe him?
2 He'll have to pay . . . this stupid mistake.
3 He received a cheque for £100 and paid it . . . to the bank.
4 She paid him . . . for the wrong he had done her.
5 It was a risky thing to do, but it paid . . . in the end.
6 He paid his servants . . . because they were not needed any longer.
7 I think you ought to pay . . . and be grateful to him for lending you the money in the first place.
8 The government pays . . . millions of pounds each year in unemployment* benefits.

# PULL

**pull about**
*vt sep\**

maltreat; handle roughly
*maltratar*

I wish you would stop *pulling* your children *about* like that.

**pull back**
*vi, vt sep*

(cause to) withdraw or retreat
*retirarse; irse*

It's doubtful whether they will ever *pull back* from the land captured in the last war.
The commander *pulled* his men *back* under cover of darkness.

**pull down**
1 *vt sep*

draw downwards
*bajar; tirar hacia abajo*

She *pulled down* the blinds* to keep the sun out.

111

**pull down**
2 *vt sep*

demolish
*derribar; demoler*

They *pulled down* the derelict* house and built a garage in its place.
Many old buildings *are being pulled down* these days.

**pull down**
3 *vt sep**

weaken; debilitate
*debilitar*

A bad attack of flu *has pulled* him *down* a lot.
She looks a bit *pulled down* by her recent illness.

**pull in(to)**
1 *vi, vt insep*

(of a train) enter a station
*(de un tren) llegar; llegar al andén*

The Orient Express *pulled in* dead on time.
It was close upon midnight when we *pulled into* Paddington.

**pull in(to)**
2 *vi, vt insep*

(of a vehicle) draw to a halt at the roadside
*(de un coche) parar (junto a la acera)*

Suddenly the car *pulled in* to the side of the road.
On our way to Cambridge we *pulled into* a lay-by* for some coffee.

**pull off**
1 *vt sep*

remove with force
*arrancar; quitarse la ropa*

He *pulled off* his jumper and started digging the garden.
She *pulled* her gloves *off* and placed them on the table.

**pull off**
2 *vt sep*

succeed in achieving sth. difficult
*concluir con éxito; llevar a cabo; conseguir*

You can rely on him to *pull off* the deal.
We *have pulled* it *off*; we have won the championship.

**pull on**
*vt sep*

don; put on
*ponerse (la ropa)*

She *pulled on* a jumper over her shirt.
He *pulled* his boots *on* and hurried off to school.

112

| | |
|---|---|
| **pull out**<br>1 *vi* | (of a train) leave a station<br>*(de un tren) salir de la estación* |
| | The train *pulled out* half an hour late.<br>Our connection to Istanbul *was pulling out* of platform six as we ran into the station. |
| **pull out**<br>2 *vi* | withdraw (from)<br>*retirarse; abandonar* |
| | If you don't *pull out* now you'll regret it later.<br>They decided *to pull out* of the bargain at the very last minute. |
| **pull out**<br>3 *vt sep* | extract<br>*sacar; arrancar* |
| | Take the pincers* and *pull* those nails *out*.<br>He has gone to the dentist to have a bad tooth *pulled out*. |
| **pull over**<br>*vi* | move to the side of the road<br>*desviarse hacia un lado; apartarse* |
| | The lorry driver *pulled over* to let us pass.<br>The car ahead of us suddenly *pulled over* and stopped. |
| **pull through**<br>*vi, vt sep*\* | recover; help recover<br>*(ayudar a) recobrar la salud; salir adelante* |
| | He was seriously injured, but managed *to pull through.*<br>She was critically ill in hospital, but good doctors and careful nursing *pulled* her *through*. |
| **pull together**<br>1 *vi* | co-operate; work in harmony<br>*cooperar; trabajar juntos* |
| | After this crushing defeat, the Party needs *to pull together* more than ever before.<br>We can come through this crisis if we all *pull together*. |

**pull together**
2 vt sep*

(with reflexive pronoun) compose oneself
*(con pronombre reflexivo) (a) animarse; (b) serenarse*

The girl had been crying, but *pulled* herself *together* when she saw me coming.
Please, George, *pull* yourself *together*.

**pull up**
1 vi, vt sep

(cause to) stop
*parar*

The car suddenly *pulled up* and two men with pistols leapt out.
He *pulled up* his car opposite the building and waited.

**pull up**
2 vt sep

uproot; pluck
*arrancar*

The gardener *pulled up* the weeds* from the flower-beds.
He *pulled* the tree *up* by the roots.

**pull up**
3 vt sep*

rebuke; reprimand
*reprender; regañar; reñir*

She *pulled* her son *up* for answering her back.
Those children ought *to be pulled up* about their bad manners.

*EXERCISE 32*

Fill in the blank spaces with the correct prepositions or particles:

1 It was getting on for one o'clock when we pulled ... Euston.
2 A lot of old houses are being pulled ... and replaced by modern blocks of flats.
3 The troops pulled ... to prepared lines of defence.
4 I should like to know who pulled ... those plants.
5 Will you help me pull ... these tight boots, please?
6 He was sharply pulled ... for his rude remarks.
7 The doctor assured me that she would pull ... all right.
8 You know I hate being pulled ... like that, so stop it.
9 Pull yourself ..., man!
10 The driver pulled ... at the traffic lights and waited.
11 He has managed to pull ... yet another important business deal.
12 You'd better pull ... before it's too late.

13 The family has always pulled ... in difficult times like these.
14 The policeman signalled to the driver to pull ... to the side of the road.
15 It was so cold outside he hurried to pull ... a warm sweater.

# PUT

**put about**
*vt sep*

spread; circulate
*dar a entender que; hacer correr el rumor de que*

Somebody has been *putting* rumours *about* that we are getting engaged.
It was *put about* that she was having an affair with her driving instructor.

**put across**
*vt sep\**

communicate; explain
*comunicar; hacer comprender*

The teacher knows his stuff\* well, but he can't *put* it *across* (to the class).
How can we best *put* our manifesto\* *across* to the electorate\*?

**put aside**
1 *vt sep*

place to one side
*poner a un lado*

She *put aside* her sewing to rest her eyes for a few minutes.
*Put* your book *aside* and listen to me carefully.

**put aside**
2 *vt sep*

ignore; disregard
*olvidar(se); pasar por alto*

I can't *put aside* the fact that the man once committed a murder.
In times of national crisis, party differences *should be put aside*.

**put aside**
3 *vt sep*

save
*ahorrar*

We've managed *to put aside* enough money for a holiday this summer.
I have a few hundred pounds *put aside* for emergencies.

115

| | |
|---|---|
| **put away**<br>1 *vt sep* | put in the proper place<br>*poner en su lugar* |

Don't leave your things about; *put* them *away*.
*Put* those papers *away* in your drawers.

| | |
|---|---|
| **put away**<br>2 *vt sep* | confine (esp. in a mental home)<br>*(a) encarcelar; (b) internar en un manicomio* |

The authorities *put* him *away* for assaulting* harmless old ladies.
A man like that deserves *to be put away* for life.

| | |
|---|---|
| **put away**<br>3 *vt sep* | devour; eat copiously<br>*comer; devorar; consumir* |

You would be surprised at the amount of food this child can *put away*.
She *put away* a huge breakfast before she left.

| | |
|---|---|
| **put away**<br>4 *vt sep* | (of animals) put to death<br>*sacrificar (un animal)* |

We decided *to put away* that dog because it was suffering too much.
The horse broke a leg and had *to be put away*.

| | |
|---|---|
| **put away**<br>5 *vt sep* | = put aside (3) |

| | |
|---|---|
| **put back**<br>1 *vt sep* | replace; return<br>*devolver (a su lugar)* |

Please *put* that dress *back* in the wardrobe.
*Put* that thing *back* where you found it.

| | |
|---|---|
| **put back**<br>2 *vt sep* | move backwards<br>*atrasar; retrasar (un reloj)* |

The clock was ten minutes fast, so I *put* it *back*.
We *put* our watches *back* by an hour.

| | |
|---|---|
| **put back**<br>3 *vt sep* | delay; hinder<br>*retrasar* |

The miners' ban* on overtime *put back* production by 15%.
This *will put* us *back* five years at least.

| | |
|---|---|
| **put by**<br>*vt sep* | = put aside (3) |

| | |
|---|---|
| **put down**<br>1 *vt sep* | place down<br>*poner (en el suelo); dejar* |

They *put down* the heavy box gently.
*Put* that gun *down*, you idiot!

| | |
|---|---|
| **put down**<br>2 *vt sep* | allow to alight; drop<br>*dejar (apearse)* |

Please *put* me *down* at the next junction.
Ask the conductor *to put* you *down* at the Albert Hall.

| | |
|---|---|
| **put down**<br>3 *vt sep* | suppress; crush; quell<br>*sofocar; aniquilar* |

The army *put down* the rebellion* with ferocity*.
The revolt* *was* savagely *put down*.

| | |
|---|---|
| **put down**<br>4 *vt sep* | record; write down<br>*apuntar; escribir* |

If I don't *put down* his address in my diary, I'm certain to forget it.
He wants everything *put down* on paper.
The instructions *were put down* in black and white.
Please *put* the drinks *down* to me/to my account.

| | |
|---|---|
| **put down**<br>5 *vt sep* | = put away (4) |

| | |
|---|---|
| **put down to**<br>*vt sep\** | attribute to; ascribe to<br>*atribuir; achacar* |

I *put* his bad performance *down to* nerves.
His poor health can be *put down to* malnutrition.

| **put forward**<br>1 *vt sep* | move forward<br>*adelantar (un reloj)* |
| | |

Your watch is a bit slow; *put* it *forward* to the correct time.
At the beginning of British summer time, clocks are *put forward* one hour.

| **put forward**<br>2 *vt sep* | advance; offer for consideration<br>*proponer; presentar* |

He *had put forward* lots of good suggestions.
The committee *has put forward* a series of proposals for settling the dispute.

| **put forward**<br>3 *vt sep* | nominate; recommend<br>*proponer (un candidato)* |

He will *put* himself *forward* as a candidate at the next election.
His was one of the names *put forward* for promotión.

| **put in**<br>1 *vt sep* | insert; add<br>*meter; introducir* |

You'll have *to put in* four 10p pieces before you can start the machine.
This article is a bit too short. Why not *put in* a few more paragraphs?

| **put in**<br>2 *vt sep* | devote; spend<br>*dedicar; invertir (tiempo) en* |

He *has put in* a lot of work on that project.
How many hours do you have *to put in* on your French each day?

| **put in**<br>3 *vi, vt insep* | apply; submit<br>*presentarse a; presentar* |

He *put in* for that job, but they turned him down.
The manager *put in* an application for extra staff in his department.

118

| | |
|---|---|
| **put off**<br>1 *vt sep* | postpone; defer<br>*aplazar; dejar (para mañana, etc)* |
| | Never *put off* till tomorrow what you can do today.<br>(proverb)<br>We shall have *to put* the meeting *off* until after Easter. |
| **put off**<br>2 *vt sep* | discourage; deter<br>*desanimar; disuadir* |
| | She wanted to do that course, but the teacher *put* her *off*<br>by saying how difficult it was.<br>Don't listen to any of that nonsense; he is only trying to<br>*put* you *off*. |
| **put off**<br>3 *vt sep* | repel; cause to dislike<br>*repugnar; dar asco a* |
| | I don't like curry; the smell *puts* me *off*.<br>His bad breath *put* me *off* my meal. |
| **put off**<br>4 *vt sep* | extinguish; switch off<br>*apagar; quitar; desconectar* |
| | Don't forget *to put off* the lights before you go to bed.<br>*Put* that wireless *off*; I can't concentrate at all. |
| **put off**<br>5 *vt sep* | get rid of by delay or evasive shifts<br>*dar largas a uno* |
| | He keeps *putting off* his creditors with promises.<br>I'm not going *to be put off* with excuses any longer. |
| **put off**<br>6 *vt sep* | disturb; distract<br>*interrumpir; molestar; distraer* |
| | Will you two keep quiet! You *are putting* me *off*.<br>The slightest thing can *put* him *off* when he is working. |
| **put off**<br>7 *vt sep* | = put down (2) |
| **put on**<br>1 *vt sep* | don; dress in<br>*ponerse (la ropa)* |
| | Take off that dirty shirt and *put on* a clean one.<br>The gentleman *put* his hat *on* when he left the house. |

119

| | |
|---|---|
| **put on**<br>2 *vt sep* | light; switch on<br>*poner; encender* |

*Put* the electric fire *on*, please; I'm feeling a bit cold.
She *put on* the radio to listen to the news.

| | |
|---|---|
| **put on**<br>3 *vt sep* | gain (weight)<br>*engordar* |

She *put on* a lot of weight over the Christmas period.
He *put on* five kilos living in the country.

| | |
|---|---|
| **put on**<br>4 *vt insep* | assume; affect<br>*fingir* |

He *put on* a posh accent to impress his visitors.
It was obvious to everybody that her grief was only *put on.*

| | |
|---|---|
| **put on**<br>5 *vt sep* | produce; stage<br>*poner en escena; representar; organizar (una fiesta)* |

The schoolchildren *put on* a show for the Queen's visit.
We usually *put* a party *on* at the end of each term.

| | |
|---|---|
| **put out**<br>1 *vt sep\** | expel; throw out<br>*expulsar* |

If you don't keep quiet you'*ll be put out* at once.

| | |
|---|---|
| **put out**<br>2 *vt sep* | extinguish<br>*apagar* |

Remember *to put out* all the lights before you go out.
The child *put* the candle *out* by blowing at it.

| | |
|---|---|
| **put out**<br>3 *vt sep\** | (*usu. pass.*) upset; annoy<br>*(normalmente en voz pasiva) molestar; enfadar* |

He was very much *put out* by her rude remarks.
Your mother feels rather *put out* about this incident.

| | |
|---|---|
| **put out**<br>4 *vt sep*\* | inconvenience or trouble (oneself)<br>*molestar; incomodar* |
| | Please don't *put* yourself *out* for me.<br>He would never *put* himself *out* for anyone, not even for you. |
| **put out**<br>5 *vt sep* | dislocate<br>*dislocarse* |
| | She fell down the ladder and *put* her shoulder *out* badly. |
| **put over**<br>*vt sep* | = put across |
| **put through**<br>1 *vt sep* | connect (by telephone)<br>*poner (en comunicación) con* |
| | If you will hold on, sir, I'll *put* you *through* to the manager.<br>*Put* me *through* to the president. It's urgent. |
| **put through**<br>2 *vt sep* | conclude; complete<br>*concluir; llevar a cabo* |
| | I'm quite confident that he'*ll put* the deal *through* without any difficulty.<br>We are hoping *to put* this scheme *through* by next March. |
| **put together**<br>*vt sep* | assemble<br>*montar* |
| | It's easier to take a clock apart than *to put* it *together* again. |
| **put up**<br>1 *vt sep* | raise<br>*levantar; alzar* |
| | He *put up* the ladder and then took it down again.<br>The pupil *put* his hand *up* to ask a question. |

121

| | |
|---|---|
| **put up**<br>2 *vt sep* | build; erect<br>*construir; montar* |

They *have put up* tower-blocks all over the town.
He is going *to put* a tent *up* in his garden.

| | |
|---|---|
| **put up**<br>3 *vi, vt sep* | lodge; give lodging to<br>*alojar; dar una habitación a* |

We *put up* at a guest-house for three nights.
Can you *put* me *up* for the night?
I shall be very glad *to put* you *up* when you come to London.

| | |
|---|---|
| **put up**<br>4 *vt sep* | increase; raise<br>*aumentar; subir (un precio)* |

The banks *have put up* their interest rates by one per cent.
The landlady has twice *put* the rent *up* in the past twelve months.

| | |
|---|---|
| **put up**<br>5 *vt insep* | provide; raise (money)<br>*proveer (dinero)* |

A generous benefactor* *put up* the money for the scheme.
You have only two days *to put up* the cash.

| | |
|---|---|
| **put up with**<br>*vt insep* | tolerate; bear; endure<br>*aguantar; tolerar* |

I refuse *to put up with* his impertinence* any longer.
We have *to put up with* a lot of noise from the neighbours.


*EXERCISE 33*

**A** Replace the underlined words with phrasal verbs containing *put*. In some examples more than one answer is possible:

1 It took the firemen several hours to extinguish the blaze.
2 He has gained weight since he stopped smoking.
3 A statue of Admiral Nelson was erected after his death.
4 Let's postpone our visit to the museum till next week.
5 I won't tolerate any bad behaviour in this house.

6 The government intends to <u>increase</u> the price of petrol by 2p a gallon.
7 She <u>donned</u> her best dress for the occasion.
8 He has <u>advanced</u> some very convincing arguments in support of the idea.
9 The speaker didn't seem to be able to <u>explain</u> his views effectively.
10 He has <u>submitted</u> a claim for travel expenses.
11 You should look ahead and try to <u>save</u> something for your retirement.
12 The boy <u>assumed</u> an air of innocence when he was accused of breaking the window.
13 Troops were called out to <u>suppress</u> the rebellion.
14 Her face is enough to <u>repel</u> anyone.
15 The accident was <u>attributed to</u> careless driving.

**B** Fill in the blank spaces with the correct prepositions or particles:

1 Put your toys . . . , darling! It's time to go to bed.
2 Your watch is ten minutes fast; you'd better put it . . . .
3 We'll have to put him . . . until he finds somewhere to live.
4 I'll put you . . . to that extension* if you will hold the line.
5 Put . . . the light, please; it's getting dark in here.
6 When you've finished with these books, remember to put them . . . on the shelf.
7 Someone has put the story . . . that the chairman is resigning.
8 I took the liberty of putting your name . . . on the list.
9 Don't put . . . your cigarette in the saucer; use the ash-tray.
10 Her husband knocks her about a lot. I'm surprised she puts . . . . . . it.

# RUN

| | |
|---|---|
| **run across**<br>*vt insep* | meet or find by chance<br>*encontrar; tropezar con* |

I *ran across* an old friend of mine in London yesterday.
Where did you *run across* these old coins?

| | |
|---|---|
| **run after**<br>*vt insep* | chase; pursue<br>*correr detrás de; seguir; perseguir* |

The shopkeeper *ran after* the thief who had stolen some goods.
She has been *running after* him for years, but he isn't interested in her.

123

| | |
|---|---|
| **run along**<br>*vi* | see *get along*, *run away* (2) example 2<br>*véase GET ALONG, RUN AWAY (2), ejemplo 2* |
| **run away**<br>1 *vi* | escape; flee<br>*huir; escaparse; evadirse* |
| | The boys *ran away* when I shouted at them.<br>This is the third time he *has run away* from school.<br>At the age of fifteen he ran away from home and went to sea*. |
| **run away**<br>2 *vi* | leave; go away<br>*irse* |
| | Don't *run away*; I have something to show you.<br>Your daddy is busy, darling; *run away* and play in the garden. |
| **run away**<br>**with**<br>1 *vt insep* | elope with<br>*fugarse con* |
| | Their son *has run away with* the neighbour's daughter.<br>She *ran away with* her music teacher. |
| **run away**<br>**with**<br>2 *vt insep* | steal and run away<br>*robar; huir con (el dinero de)* |
| | While I was having coffee in the cafeteria, someone *ran away with* my luggage.<br>The cashier *has run away with* the company's money. |
| **run away**<br>**with**<br>3 *vt insep* | consume; use up<br>*devorar; tragar* |
| | These big cars *run away with* a lot of petrol.<br>A project of this magnitude will *run away with* our funds. |
| **run away**<br>**with**<br>4 *vt insep* | accept (an idea) too hastily<br>*imaginarse; meter una idea en la cabeza* |
| | Don't *run away with* the idea that you are indispensable*. |

124

| | |
|---|---|
| **run away**<br>**with**<br>5 *vt insep* | gain complete control of<br>*dejarse llevar por/de* |
| | He tends to let his temper *run away with* him.<br>Don't let your enthusiasm *run away with* you. |
| **run away**<br>**with**<br>6 *vt insep* | win easily<br>*ganar facilmente* |
| | Their candidate* *ran away with* the election.<br>The Chinese players *ran away with* the table-tennis tournament*. |
| **run back**<br>*vt sep* | re-wind (film, tape, etc.)<br>*rebobinar; volver atrás (una cinta, etc)* |
| | I'll *run* the tape *back* when I've finished listening to it.<br>Can we have that bit of the film *run back*, please? |
| **run down**<br>1 *vi* | become unwound or discharged<br>*pararse (un reloj); descargarse o acabarse (una pila)* |
| | The clock *ran down* because I forgot to wind it.<br>The batteries seem to *have run down.* |
| **run down**<br>2 *vt sep* | knock down with a vehicle<br>*atropellar* |
| | A careless driver *ran* her *down* as she was crossing the street.<br>He was *run down* by a taxi and was rushed to hospital. |
| **run down**<br>3 *vt sep* | disparage; speak ill of<br>*hablar mal de; denigrar a; murmurar de* |
| | He is always *running down* his colleagues behind their backs. |
| **run down**<br>4 *vt sep* | find; locate<br>*encontrar; localizar* |
| | The police finally *ran* him *down* at a small hotel in Paris.<br>We've had an awful lot of trouble *running* her *down.* |

| | |
|---|---|
| **run down**<br>5 *vt sep* | (*pass.*) exhausted; debilitated<br>*(voz pasiva) agotado; exhausto; debilitado* |
| | You look terribly *run down*, George. I think you ought to take a long holiday.<br>I don't know what's the matter with me, but I feel completely *run down*. |
| **run for**<br>*vt insep* | be a candidate for<br>*ser candidato; presentarse como candidato* |
| | He *ran for* Mayor twice, but was unsuccessful on both occasions.<br>He has finally made up his mind *to run for* President. |
| **run in**<br>1 *vt sep* | drive (a new car) slowly and carefully to avoid straining the engine<br>*rodar (un coche) (*running in – *en rodaje)* |
| | If you want *to run in* your car properly you shouldn't exceed 35 miles an hour.<br>'*Running in.* Please pass.' (notice on the back window of a new car) |
| **run in**<br>2 *vt sep* | arrest; apprehend<br>*detener; meter en la cárcel* |
| | The police *ran* him *in* for indecent\* exposure.<br>Brian *was run in* for speeding last night. |
| **run into**<br>1 *vt insep* | collide with<br>*chocar con; dar con;* |
| | She lost control of her car and *ran into* a stationary\* van.<br>The two planes *ran into* each other on the runway\*. |
| **run into**<br>2 *vt insep* | meet by chance<br>*encontrar; tropezar con* |
| | I *ran into* an old school friend on a visit to Edinburgh. |
| **run into**<br>3 *vt insep* | amount to; reach<br>*alcanzar; ascender a* |
| | His annual\* income *runs into* five figures.<br>Her new book *has run into* three impressions\* already. |

| | |
|---|---|
| **run into**<br>4 *vt insep* | be involved in<br>*contraer (deudas); meterse en; tener (dificultades)* |
| | You'll soon *run into* debt if you are not careful with your spending.<br>I'm afraid your son *has run into* trouble with the headmaster. |
| **run off with**<br>*vt insep* | = run away with (1), (2) |
| **run out**<br>1 *vi* | come to an end<br>*agotarse; acabarse* |
| | What are we going to do when our supply of food *runs out*?<br>My patience is beginning *to run out*. |
| **run out**<br>2 *vi* | expire; terminate<br>*caducar; expirar* |
| | My driving-licence *runs out* on November 18th.<br>When does your contract *run out*? |
| **run out of**<br>*vt insep* | exhaust; finish completely<br>*quedarse sin algo* |
| | We *ran out of* petrol in the middle of nowhere.<br>We *are running out of* time, gentlemen!<br>I *have run out of* ideas; I can't think of anything. |
| **run over**<br>1 *vi, vt insep* | overflow<br>*desbordar; derramarse; rebosar* |
| | I forgot to turn off the taps in the bath, and the water *ran over*.<br>The milk *has run* all *over* the floor. |
| **run over**<br>2 *vt insep* | recapitulate; rehearse<br>*volver a hacer; resumir; repasar (lecciones)* |
| | I'll just *run over* the main points of the lesson again.<br>Let us *run over* that bit once more, shall we? |

127

| | |
|---|---|
| **run over**<br>3 *vt sep* | go over while driving<br>*atropellar* |
| | Look out! You nearly *ran over* that woman.<br>He *was run over* by a car and killed instantly. |
| **run through**<br>1 *vt insep* | read or examine quickly<br>*repasar; hojear* |
| | Just *run through* this essay and tell me what you think of it.<br>The teacher *ran through* his notes before starting the lesson. |
| **run through**<br>2 *vt insep* | spend completely; squander<br>*despilfarrar; gastar* |
| | He has already *run through* the money he inherited from his uncle.<br>She *ran through* the fortune in less than a year. |
| **run through**<br>3 *vt sep** | impale; pierce<br>*traspasar; atravesar* |
| | He *ran* his enemy *through* with a sword.<br>The sentries* *were run through* with spears. |
| **run to**<br>1 *vt insep* | amount to; reach<br>*(a) alcanzar; extenderse a; (b) sumar; ascender a* |
| | The repair bill *will run to* several thousand pounds.<br>His dissertation* *runs to* approximately four hundred pages. |
| **run to**<br>2 *vt insep* | be sufficient for; afford<br>*tener bastante dinero para; permitirse el lujo de* |
| | My salary won't *run to* eating in expensive restaurants.<br>I can't possibly *run to* a new colour TV. |
| **run up**<br>1 *vt sep* | raise; hoist<br>*izar* |
| | The besieged garrison *ran up* a white flag as a sign of surrender. |

| run up | accumulate |
|---|---|
| 2 *vt sep* | *contraer (deudas); acumular* |

She *ran up* a large bill at the butcher's.
You *have run up* an awful lot of debts already.

| run up | sew quickly |
|---|---|
| 3 *vt sep* | *hacer de prisa* |

My sister *ran up* that blouse for me this morning.
It shouldn't take long *to run up* this dress.

| run up against | encounter; meet with |
|---|---|
| *vt insep* | *encontrar; tropezar con* |

We did not expect *to run up against* that kind of opposition.
He *has run up against* all sorts of problems.


## EXERCISE 34

**A**  Fill in the blank spaces with the correct prepositions or particles. In some examples more than one answer is possible.

1 We have run . . . . . . sugar. Will you go and buy some?
2 Don't run . . . . . . the idea that you can go on breaking the rules.
3 She was run . . . by a cyclist and broke her arm.
4 He is looking a bit run . . . after his illness.
5 Two small boys ran . . . . . . my handbag and disappeared in the crowd.
6 I ran . . . Hilda at a fun-fair* the other day.
7 She is inclined to let her imagination run . . . . . . her.
8 The car skidded* and ran . . . the back of a lorry.
9 It's almost impossible to run . . . from this prison.
10 The budget* just won't run . . . caviare every day.
11 My wife is running . . . accounts at five different shops.
12 You will ruin your car if you do not run it . . . properly.

**B**  Use synonyms in place of the underlined phrasal verbs:

1 She is always <u>running</u> her neighbours <u>down</u>.
2 The police <u>ran him in</u> for dangerous driving.
3 Let us just <u>run through</u> this part one more time.
4 This is just one of the obstacles* we expect to <u>run up against</u>.
5 She <u>ran off with</u> a man old enough to be her father.

6 The policeman <u>ran after</u> the thief, but could not catch him.
7 The present agreement <u>runs out</u> in June.
8 This scheme will simply <u>run away with</u> our money.
9 It took me the whole afternoon to <u>run down</u> the reference.
10 Time is <u>running out</u>, and so we must hurry.
11 Don't put too much water in the tank, or it'll <u>run over</u>.
12 She has already <u>run through</u> the fortune she won on the pools.

# SEE

**see about**
*vt insep*

attend to; deal with (see *see to*)
*ocuparse de; atender a*

When are you going *to see about* those bills? They should have been paid a month ago, you know!
We must *see about* decorating the spare room for auntie's visit.

**see into**
*vt insep*

investigate; inquire into
*investigar; examinar*

He promised that he would *see into* the matter at once.
Perhaps you wouldn't mind *seeing into* it for me then?

**see off**
1 *vt sep\**

accompany sb. to his point of departure
*ir a despedir a uno*

They have gone to the airport *to see* their daughter *off*.
He *was seen off* by some of his relatives and close friends.

**see off**
2 *vt sep\**

cause to leave
*echar; poner de patitas en la calle*

I don't like those men hanging about the place; please *see* them *off* (the premises\*).

**see out**
1 *vt sep.\**

conduct to the door
*acompañar a la puerta*

Miss Brown, *will* you *see* this lady *out*, please?
Don't bother to get up; I can *see* myself *out*.

**see out**
**2** *vt sep\**
live or last until a specified period has elapsed
*resistir; durar*

It's doubtful whether he *will see* another week *out*.
Do we have enough coal *to see* the winter *out*?

**see over**
*vt insep*
inspect
*visitar; examinar*

They went *to see over* the house yesterday, but they didn't find it very attractive.

**see through**
**1** *vt insep*
understand the true nature of sb. or his dubious intentions
*calar a uno; adivinar la intención de*

She thought she could fool me, but I *saw through* her game immediately.
I *saw through* him at once. I knew exactly what he was after.

**see through**
**2** *vt sep\**
bring to a conclusion
*llevar a cabo; concluir*

We are still hoping that you will be able *to see* the work *through* by next spring.
You can rely on him *to see* this thing *through*.

**see through**
**3** *vt sep\**
help sb. through a difficult time
*ayudar; echar una mano*

He had always trusted that his friends *would see* him *through* when he was in trouble.
I hope this small cheque *will see* you *through*.

**see to**
*vt insep*
attend to; take care of
*encargarse de; asegurarse de que*

I'*ll see to* it you receive the cheque within the next few days.
*See to* it that Mr Freeman is not disturbed.
The lift has broken down again. Have it *seen to* at once.

Fill in the blank spaces with the correct prepositions or particles. In some examples more than one answer is possible:

1 I'll do the washing-up if you'll see . . . the dinner.
2 A good host always sees his guests . . . when they leave.
3 You are leaving tomorrow, are you? I'll come and see you . . . at the station.
4 You must see . . . booking* seats for the play before they are sold out.
5 Take the dog and see those trespassers . . . my land.
6 I'm not such a fool, you know! I can see . . . your clever plans.
7 A party of foreign visitors came to see . . . the factory this morning.
8 They are determined to see their struggle . . . right to the end.
9 I wonder whether granny will see the month . . . . She looks very ill.
10 We are seeing . . . the question of extending his contract for a further six months.

# SET

| | |
|---|---|
| **set about**<br>1 *vt insep* | begin; tackle<br>*ponerse a; emprender* |

They *set about* their work eagerly.
He doesn't have the slightest idea of how *to set about* the job.
As soon as the ship entered dock* they *set about* unloading the cargo*.

| | |
|---|---|
| **set about**<br>2 *vt insep* | attack<br>*atacar; agredir* |

The two boys *set about* each other fiercely.
The policemen *set about* some demonstrators with their clubs*.

| | |
|---|---|
| **set apart**<br>*vt sep** | cause to stand out<br>*separar; hacer destacar; distinguir* |

His intelligence *sets* him *apart* from the rest of the class.

| | |
|---|---|
| **set aside**<br>1 *vt sep* | place to one side<br>*poner a un lado; dejar* |
| | She *set aside* her knitting when I came into the room.<br>He *set* his paper *aside* and listened to what she had to say. |
| **set aside**<br>2 *vt sep* | disregard; dismiss<br>*olvidar; rechazar; desechar* |
| | You must look at this objectively and *set aside* your personal feelings.<br>The speaker *set aside* all objections made by some people in the audience. |
| **set aside**<br>3 *vt sep* | annul; quash<br>*anular; rechazar* |
| | The appeal court *set aside* the judgement of the lower court.<br>The verdict of the jury *was set aside* and the death sentence commuted*. |
| **set aside**<br>4 *vt sep* | see *put aside/by* |
| **set back**<br>1 *vt sep* | move backwards<br>*atrasar (un reloj)* |
| | He *set back* the hands of the clock one hour. |
| **set back**<br>2 *vt sep* | hinder; delay<br>*costar (tiempo); impedir; detener (el progreso)* |
| | The continuing industrial disputes could *set back* our economic recovery considerably.<br>This *will set* us *back* some years. |
| **set back**<br>3 *vt sep** | cost<br>*costar* |
| | His birthday party *set* him *back* hundreds of pounds.<br>That new car must *have set* him *back* quite a bit. |
| **set down**<br>1 *vt sep* | allow to alight; drop<br>*dejar* |
| | The taxi *set* us *down* just opposite the museum.<br>Could you please *set* me *down* at the next set of lights? |

133

**set down**
2 *vt sep*

record; write down
*escribir; apuntar*

He asked me *to set* everything *down* on paper.
The instructions *were set down* in black and white.

**set forth**
*vt sep*

expound; give an account of
*exponer; explicar*

The minister *set forth* his views with clarity and force.
The Liberal leader *set forth* the policies of his party in an
interview with newspaper reporters.

**set in**
*vi*

begin; start
*empezar (de verdad)*

Winter *set in* rather early this year.
The rain seems *to have set in* for the night.

**set off**
1 *vi*

depart; begin a journey
*partir; ponerse en camino*

We intend *to set off* tomorrow at dawn.
They *have set off* on an expedition* to the Antarctic.*
They *set off* for Australia in great haste.

**set off**
2 *vt sep*

cause to explode
*hacer estallar*

Some boys *were setting off* fireworks in the street.
The terrorists* *set* a bomb *off* outside the shopping
precinct.

**set off**
3 *vt sep*

cause to start
*hacer empezar algo; causar*

His latest book *has set off* a fierce controversy.*
That remark *set* everybody *off* laughing.

**set off**
4 *vt sep*

intensify or improve by contrast
*poner de relieve; hacer resaltar; acentuar; realzar*

This ring, madam, *will set off* your hand beautifully.
Her black hair *was set off* by the red dress she was wearing.

134

| | |
|---|---|
| **set on**<br>*vt insep* | attack<br>*atacar* |
| | As he was walking down the street one night, two men suddenly *set on* him and knocked him senseless.<br>He *was set on* and beaten up by a gang of boys. |
| **set out**<br>1 *vi* | = set off (1) |
| **set out**<br>2 *vi* | have as an intention or goal<br>*tener la intención de; proponerse* |
| | She *set out* to become the first woman prime minister.<br>This article *sets out* to prove that smoking is the main cause of lung cancer.* |
| **set out**<br>3 *vt sep* | state; explain<br>*exponer; explicar* |
| | He *set out* his arguments in a remarkably convincing way.<br>The Liberals *have set out* their conditions for supporting the government in tomorrow's no-confidence vote.* |
| **set out**<br>4 *vt sep* | organize; display<br>*(a) disponer; (b) organizar* |
| | You haven't *set out* your essay very well, I'm afraid.<br>The goods *were* neatly *set out* on the stalls. |
| **set to**<br>1 *vi* | begin to work vigorously<br>*ponerse a trabajar; aplicarse a* |
| | They *set to* and finished the job in no time at all. |
| **set to**<br>2 *vi* | begin to fight or argue<br>*empezar a pegarse/discutir; enzarzarse (en una pelea)* |
| | The two men *set to* with their fists. |

**set up**
1 *vi*

start a business
*establecerse*

At the end of the war, his father moved to Bournemouth where he *set up* as an inn-keeper.

**set up**
2 *vt sep*

erect; place in position
*levantar; montar*

He *set up* a hot-dog\* stall outside the football stadium.
The army *set up* an observation post at the top of the hill.

**set up**
3 *vt sep*

establish; institute
*establecer; constituir*

The government *has set up* a commission\* to examine the country's educational system.
An inquiry into the causes of the air crash *was set up* by the airline officials.

**set up**
4 *vi, vt sep\**

claim to be
*hacer creer que uno es; dárselas de*

I do not *set up* to be an expert in this field.
He *sets* himself *up* as an authority on fossils.\*

**set up**
5 *vt sep*

achieve (a record)
*establecer*

The Russian athletes *set up* several new records at the last Olympic Games.

**set up**
6 *vt sep*

provide; equip
*proveer; dar; proporcionar*

His parents *set* him *up* with the necessary books for college.
The children *have been set up* with all the clothes they need.

Fill in the blank spaces with the correct prepositions or particles. In some examples more than one answer is possible:

1 Ask the driver to set you ... at the Odeon.
2 They set ... their reasons for refusing to support the motion⁺.
3 The League* of Nations was set ... in 1919.
4 This frame will set ... your painting very nicely.
5 A rare talent set Shakespeare ... from other Elizabethan poets.
6 We must get the shed fixed before the bad weather sets ....
7 They have been set ... with all the provisions they need for the voyage.
8 I don't know how to set ... a job like this.
9 He set ... to break the world record for the high jump.
10 We set ... at five and reached our destination before sunset.
11 The dinner set me ... eight quid*.
12 The policeman set ... in writing all the statements we made.
13 A gang of hooligans* set ... him and injured him very badly.
14 The recent outbreaks of violence could set ... the peace efforts considerably.
15. He gave up his job at the factory and set ... as a greengrocer.

# SHOW

**show (a)round**  take sb. round a place
  *vt sep*     *enseñar*

          I'd love *to show* you *around* the city.
          We *were shown round* the factory by the director himself.

**show in(to)**  usher into a place
  *vt sep*     *hacer pasar; hacer entrar*

          When Mr Francis arrives *show* him *in* at once.
          The secretary *showed* me *into* the manager's office.
          We *were shown into* a large drawing-room by the butler*.

**show off**  boast; behave ostentatiously
  1 *vi*     *presumir; darse importancia; hacerse notar*

          He just can't help *showing off* in public.
          I wish you would stop *showing off*, William!

| | | |
|---|---|---|
| **show off**<br>2 *vt sep* | exhibit; display<br>*hacer resaltar; poner de relieve; realzar* | |

This dress *shows off* your figure very nicely.
The gold frame *shows* the painting *off* well.

| | | |
|---|---|---|
| **show off**<br>3 *vt sep* | display ostentatiously<br>*lucir* | |

She went to the dance just *to show off* her new clothes.
She likes *to show* her daughter *off*, doesn't she?

| | | |
|---|---|---|
| **show out**<br>*vt sep* | conduct to the door<br>*acompañar a la puerta* | |

Miss Perkins, will you *show* this gentleman *out*, please?
The guests *were shown out* by the maid.

| | | |
|---|---|---|
| **show up**<br>1 *vi* | arrive; appear<br>*acudir; llegar; aparecer* | |

I can't understand why she hasn't *shown up* yet.
He never *shows up* on time for these meetings.
Only twenty people *showed up* at the party.

| | | |
|---|---|---|
| **show up**<br>2 *vt sep* | expose; unmask<br>*desenmascarar; revelar; descubrir* | |

He obviously enjoys *showing up* other people's mistakes.
They *showed* him *up* to be an impostor*.

| | | |
|---|---|---|
| **show up**<br>3 *vt sep* | embarrass; shame<br>*humillar; avergonzar; poner en evidencia* | |

If you don't stop *showing* me *up* in public I'll never go with you anywhere.

## EXERCISE 37

Fill in the blank spaces with the correct prepositions or particles:

1 I waited for her for nearly one hour, but she didn't show . . . .
2 Don't keep the young lady waiting. Show her . . . .
3 The guide showed the tourists . . . the ancient cathedral.
4 He'll probably stop showing . . . if we don't take any notice of him.
5 My secretary will show you . . . . . It's easy to get lost in this big building.

138

6 He keeps using French words just to show ... his knowledge of the language.
7 You shouldn't have shown your mother ... in front of all those people.


# STAND

**stand about**
*vi*

stand idly in a certain place
*quedarse sin hacer nada; esperar*

He kept us *standing about* for hours.
I wish you would stop *standing about* and do something useful instead.

**stand around**
*vi*

= stand about

**stand aside**
1 *vi*

get out of the way
*apartarse; quitarse de en medio*

Will you please *stand aside* and let me pass.

**stand aside**
2 *vi*

take no part; do nothing
*no tomar parte; mantenerse al margen*

We can't *stand aside* and let him do it all by himself.
Surely you don't expect me *to stand aside* and allow this thing to happen.

**stand back**
*vi*

stand clear
*apartarse; echarse hacia atrás*

The firemen ordered the spectators* *to stand back.*
Will everybody please *stand back*!

**stand by**
1   *vi*

be a mere bystander
*no hacer nada; mantenerse al margen*

Several people *stood by* while the two men were fighting.
We cannot *stand* idly *by* and watch people die of starvation*.

139

| | |
|---|---|
| **stand by**<br>2 *vi* | be in a state of readiness<br>*mantenerse listo; estar dispuesto* |

Police were ordered *to stand by* for action.
Other troops *are standing by* to help.
*Stand by* for further instructions.

| | |
|---|---|
| **stand by**<br>3 *vt insep* | support; remain loyal to<br>*apoyar; defender* |

He had always *stood by* his friends whenever they were in trouble.
They *stood by* one another through* thick and thin.

| | |
|---|---|
| **stand by**<br>4 *vt insep* | keep; adhere to; abide by<br>*atenerse a; cumplir; mantener* |

He is not the sort of man who *stands by* his promises.
We've signed the agreement and we'*ll* just *have to stand by* it.

| | |
|---|---|
| **stand down**<br>1 *vi* | leave the witness box<br>*retirarse* |

The magistrate asked the witness *to stand down.*
You may *stand down* now!

| | |
|---|---|
| **stand down**<br>2 *vi* | withdraw (in favour of sb. else)<br>*retirarse; ceder su puesto a* |

The candidate has offered *to stand down* in favour of a younger man.
He is not going *to stand down* for anybody.

| | |
|---|---|
| **stand for**<br>1 *vt insep* | represent; mean<br>*significar; querer decir* |

USSR *stands for* Union of Soviet Socialist Republics.
The letters RAF *stand for* Royal Air Force.

| | |
|---|---|
| **stand for**<br>2 *vt insep* | (*usu. neg.*) tolerate; permit<br>*(normalmente negativo) permitir; tolerar* |

Father wouldn't *stand for* any of that nonsense.
I won't *stand for* his impudence any longer.

140

| | |
|---|---|
| **stand for**<br>3 *vt insep* | advocate; contend for<br>*ser partidario de; apoyar* |

Abraham Lincoln *stood for* the abolition of slavery in the United States.
He *has* always *stood for* racial equality.

| | |
|---|---|
| **stand for**<br>4 *vt insep* | be a candidate for<br>*ser candidato; presentarse como candidato* |

He *stood for* Parliament in 1970, but was not elected.
At the last election he *stood for* Bristol.

| | |
|---|---|
| **stand in for**<br>*vt insep* | take the place of<br>*suplir; reemplazar* |

He *had to stand in for* the actor who had been taken ill.
Will you *stand in for* me while I go out to the bank to cash a cheque?

| | |
|---|---|
| **stand off**<br>*vi* | keep at a distance<br>*apartarse; alejarse de* |

The two ships *were standing off* from each other.
The fleet* *stood off* from the shore.

| | |
|---|---|
| **stand out**<br>*vi* | be conspicuous; be prominent<br>*destacarse* |

The mosque *stood out* clearly against the sky.
He *stood out* from his contemporaries* by virtue* of his exceptional talents.

| | |
|---|---|
| **stand out against**<br>*vt insep* | persist in opposition or resistance<br>*oponerse a* |

The students *are standing out against* any further cuts in their grants*.
It takes courage *to stand out against* intimidation*.

| | |
|---|---|
| **stand over**<br>1 *vi* | wait; be postponed<br>*aplazar; dejar por el momento* |

The last item on the agenda *will have to stand over* until our next meeting.

| | |
|---|---|
| **stand over**<br>2 *vt insep* | watch closely<br>*vigilar a uno; velar a uno* |
| | I *have to stand over* him to make sure he studies.<br>Unless you *stand over* him he'll make a mess of the job. |
| **stand up**<br>*vi* | rise to the feet<br>*levantarse; ponerse de pie* |
| | The pupils *stood up* when the headmaster entered the classroom.<br>You can see better if you *stand up*. |
| **stand up for**<br>*vt insep* | defend; support<br>*defender; apoyar* |
| | Do you always *stand up for* your rights?<br>I hope you are not going *to stand up for* that rogue*. |
| **stand up to**<br>1 *vt insep* | withstand; resist<br>*resistir a* |
| | Steel *stands up to* heat better than other metals.<br>These shoes *will stand up to* a lot of wear and tear. |
| **stand up to**<br>2 *vt insep* | face boldly<br>*hacer frente a; resistir a* |
| | Stop behaving like a coward and *stand up to* him.<br>She *would stand up to* the devil himself. |

*EXERCISE 38*

A Replace the underlined words with phrasal verbs containing *stand*:

1 We dislike Nazism and all that it represents.
2 An honest man always keeps his word.
3 This matter will have to wait until later.
4 He says he is willing to withdraw if you want the job.
5 I won't tolerate this sort of behaviour.
6 Robin is taking the place of the player who has broken his leg.
7 He resisted all attempts to persuade him to change his mind.
8 What does the abbreviation *A.D.* mean?
9 These children need someone to watch them closely all the time; otherwise they never do any work.
10 This type of machine can withstand even the roughest treatment.

**B** Fill in the blank spaces with the correct prepositions or particles:

1 Don't be afraid of standing ...... that bully*.
2 Do you mean to say that you just stood ... and watched the girl drown?
3 He is thinking of standing ... mayor at the next municipal* election.
4 The pilot was instructed to stand ... and wait for final clearance before take-off.
5 She just stood ... doing nothing while I did all the cleaning.
6 He stood ... and let the others decide the question.
7 All our friends stood ... us when we most needed them.
8 Mother would always stand ...... Robert if any of us criticized him.
9 The judge asked the witness to stand ... when he had finished giving evidence.
10 He stands ... in a crowd because of his height and bald head.

# TAKE

| | |
|---|---|
| **be taken aback**<br>*vt sep** | be startled; be surprised<br>*quedar desconcertado* |

When I saw him lying so still I *was* quite *taken aback*. I really thought he was dead.
We *were* all *taken aback* by the news of his resignation.

| | |
|---|---|
| **take after**<br>*vt insep* | resemble; behave like<br>*parecerse a; salir a (una persona)* |

These children really *take after* their mother.
You certainly seem *to take after* your grandfather; he was very obstinate*, too.

| | |
|---|---|
| **take apart**<br>*vt sep** | dismantle; take to pieces<br>*desmontar; deshacer* |

He *took* the radio *apart* and then put it together again.
The mechanic *took* the engine *apart* before repairing it.

| | |
|---|---|
| **take aside**<br>*vt sep** | take to one side<br>*llevar a un lado* |

*Take* the girl *aside* and break the news gently.
He *took* me *aside* and whispered a few words in my ear about a proposed deal.

| | |
|---|---|
| **take away**<br>1 *vt sep* | remove<br>*quitar; llevarse* |

I won't need this ladder again; please *take* it *away*.
*Take* the knife *away* from that boy before he hurts himself.
In the reading rooms, books are not *to be taken away*.

| | |
|---|---|
| **take away**<br>2 *vt sep* | subtract<br>*restar* |

*Take away* 4 from 9 and you get 5.
9 *take away* 4 is 5.

| | |
|---|---|
| **take back**<br>1 *vt sep* | return<br>*devolver* |

Will you do me a favour, Jim? *Take* these books *back* (to the library).

| | |
|---|---|
| **take back**<br>2 *vt sep* | agree to receive back<br>*aceptar algo devuelto* |

The shirt which you sold me is too small. Will you *take* it *back*?
The shopkeeper refused *to take back* the rotten eggs.

| | |
|---|---|
| **take back**<br>3 *vt sep* | retract; withdraw<br>*retractarse de algo; retirar* |

I *take back* what I said yesterday, and I hope you will accept my apology.
When she found out the truth, she came to me and *took* her remarks *back*.

| | |
|---|---|
| **take back**<br>4 *vt sep*\* | remind of earlier times<br>*recordarle algo a uno; recordarle el pasado a uno* |

Those pictures *took* me *back* to the war.
This kind of music *does take* one *back*, doesn't it?

144

| | |
|---|---|
| **take down** 1 *vt sep* | get or remove from a high level *bajar; descolgar* |

She reached up to the top shelf and *took down* an atlas.
He *took down* all the pictures from the walls when the room was being painted.

| | |
|---|---|
| **take down** 2 *vt sep* | demolish; pull down *derribar* |

We are going *to take down* that partition and convert* the two small rooms into one big flat.

| | |
|---|---|
| **take down** 3 *vt sep* | record; write down *escribir; apuntar* |

The policeman *took down* all the statements I made.
You are not supposed *to take down* every word I say.

| | |
|---|---|
| **take down** 4 *vt sep* | dismantle *desmontar; desarmar* |

The builders *took down* the scaffolding* round the building.

| | |
|---|---|
| **take down** 5 *vt sep** | humble; humiliate *bajarle los humos a uno; humillar* |

That young fellow is always bragging* about himself; he needs *to be taken down* a peg or two.

| | |
|---|---|
| **take for** *vt sep** | believe or assume to be *tomar a uno por;crecr que una persona es; confundir con* |

I *took* her *for* her sister; they are very much alike.
Who *do* you *take* me *for*?
*Do* you *take* me *for* a fool?

| | |
|---|---|
| **take from** *vt insep* | detract from *quitar el valor de; quitar mérito de* |

He may have been a Nazi, but that doesn't *take from* his achievement as a physicist.

**take in**
1 *vt sep*

receive and accomodate; shelter
*recibir en su casa; alojar; llevar a casa*

The Joneses earn a bit of extra money by *taking in* lodgers.
They *took* the stray* dog *in* and fed him.

**take in**
2 *vt sep*

make narrower (a garment)
*estrechar (un vestido)*

She has lost so much weight that she *had to take in* all her dresses.
These trousers need *taking in* a little at the waist.

**take in**
3 *vt insep*

cover; comprise
*abarcar; comprender*

This package* tour *takes in* five Mediterranean countries.
Greater London *takes in* parts of several counties.

**take in**
4 *vt sep*

understand; grasp
*entender; comprender*

He is so dull-witted* that he can't *take in* even the most straightforward speech.
Did you *take in* what the man said? I didn't.

**take in**
5 *vt sep*

deceive; trick; cheat
*engañar; estafar*

You really think you can *take* me *in* with your silly stories.
The poor woman *was taken in* by the salesman and got nothing worth the money she had paid.

**take off**
1 *vi*

(of a plane) leave the ground
*(de un avión) despegar*

The aircraft crashed five minutes after it *had taken off*.
We *took off* from Heathrow Airport at 9.30 p.m.

146

| | | |
|---|---|---|
| **take off**<br>2 *vt sep* | remove<br>*quitarse (la ropa)* | |

She hurriedly *took off* her coat and sank into an armchair.
*Take* that dirty jacket *off* and put on a clean one.
He *took off* his hat when he came into the house.

| | | |
|---|---|---|
| **take off**<br>3 *vt sep* | deduct (see *knock off*)<br>*descontar; rebajar* | |

I'll stick my neck* out and *take off* five pounds just for you.
The shopkeeper *took* ten per cent *off* the bill, because I paid him in cash.

| | | |
|---|---|---|
| **take off**<br>4 *vt sep* | mimic; imitate<br>*imitar; remedar* | |

The comedian *took off* several well-known politicians during his act.
Alice *takes* the headmistress *off* to perfection.

| | | |
|---|---|---|
| **take on**<br>1 *vt sep* | employ; hire; engage<br>*emplear; contratar* | |

As they couldn't finish the work on time, they *had to take on* extra employees.
We can't *take on* any more staff, simply because we don't have the money for it.

| | | |
|---|---|---|
| **take on**<br>2 *vt sep* | accept; undertake<br>*aceptar* | |

I'm sorry to have to disappoint you, but I can't *take on* any more work this week.
You should never *have taken* this job *on* in the first place.

| | | |
|---|---|---|
| **take on**<br>3 *vt sep* | accept as an opponent<br>*desafiar; jugar contra* | |

He is ready *to take on* anybody at chess*.
I *took* Jim *on* at billiards and beat him.

147

**take on**
4 *vt insep*

acquire; assume
*asumir; tomar*

This word is beginning *to take on* a new meaning.
Her face *took on* an angry look when I said that her hat did not suit her.

**take out**
1 *vt sep\**

escort sb. somewhere for exercise or recreation
*(a) salir con (una chica); (b) llevar de paseo (un perro)*

The nurse *takes* the children *out* every day.
He *took* his girlfriend *out* to a discotheque.
I usually *take* the dog *out* for a walk after supper.

**take out**
2 *vt sep*

extract; pull out
*extraer; sacar*

.That tooth has given you so much pain. Why not see a dentist and *have* it *taken out*
She was admitted to hospital last Monday and had her appendix\* *taken out*.

**take out**
3 *vt sep*

remove (stains, etc.)
*quitar (una mancha, etc)*

This new washing-powder is very good for *taking out* all kinds of stains.

**take out**
4 *vt sep*

obtain; apply for and get
*obtener (un permiso); contratar/sacar (un seguro)*

You'll *have to take out* a driving-licence before you can drive the car.
You must *take out* an insurance policy, for the sake of your family.

**take out**
5 *vt sep\**

vent; get rid of
*desahogar (la ira, etc)*

I appreciate that you're having a difficult time, but please don't *take* your temper *out* on me.
She *took* her rage *out* on the poor dog.

148

| **take over** | assume control of |
| *vi, vt insep* | *(a) asumir el poder; tomar posesión de; (b) suplir; reemplazar* |

You've done your share of the work; now it's my turn *to take over* (from you).
When the father died, his eldest son *took over* the management of the property.
The army overthrew the old monarch and *took over* power.

| **take to** | become fond of; like |
| 1 *vt insep* | *tomar cariño a; aficionarse a* |

I *took to* that girl the moment I saw her.
I did watch bull-fighting on a couple of occasions, but I don't think I could ever *take to* it.

| **take to** | seek refuge in |
| 2 *vt insep* | *refugiarse en; recurrir a* |

Robin Hood *took to* the woods when he was made an outlaw*.
The crew could not keep the ship afloat and *took to* the life boats.

| **take to** | get into the habit of |
| 3 *vt insep* | *aficionarse a* |

He *took to* gambling when he was young and never got out of it.
Our new teacher *has taken to* wearing jeans.

| **take up** | shorten (a garment) (*cf. let down*) |
| 1 *vt sep* | *acortar (un vestido) (vease LET DOWN)* |

These trousers are too long; get the tailor *to take* them *up*.
The dress does fit you nicely, but it needs *to be taken up* an inch or so.

| **take up** | occupy; fill |
| 2 *vt sep* | *ocupar* |

Her charity work *takes up* most of her spare time.
I think we should sell that cupboard; it *takes up* too much room.

| take up<br>3 *vt sep* | raise, discuss<br>*mencionar; discutir* |
|---|---|
| | I shall certainly *take* this matter *up* with the minister himself. |
| take up<br>4 *vt insep* | adopt the practice or study of<br>*dedicarse a; aficionarse a* |
| | When my father retired, he *took up* gardening.<br>I'm thinking of *taking up* medicine when I finish secondary school. |
| take up<br>5 *vt insep* | resume; continue<br>*continuar; reanudar* |
| | He *took up* the tale from where he had left off. |
| take up with<br>*vt insep* | begin to associate with<br>*relacionarse con; hacer amistad con* |
| | I'm afraid your daughter *has taken up with* a bad lot*.<br>We don't want our son *to take up with* those boys because they are bad company. |

*EXERCISE 39*

A  Fill in the blank spaces with the correct prepositions or particles:

1  He did not recognize me in the dark and took me . . . a thief.
2  She took . . . her shoes before lying down on the bed.
3  The new director will take . . . on January 12th.
4  He took his fiancée* . . . to dinner on her birthday.
5  The watchmaker took the clock . . . before mending it.
6  His arrogant* behaviour had annoyed me for so long that I finally decided to take him . . . .
7  This new sweater of yours has a big hole in it. I'd take it . . . to the shop if I were you.
8  He took . . . life in the army like a duck to water.
9  Many old buildings are being taken . . . and replaced by modern ones.
10  He took . . . a patent* in order to protect his invention.
11  The lecture was too difficult for me to take . . . .
12  I think you ought to take . . . French; it'll help you a lot in your career.

**B** Replace the underlined words with phrasal verbs containing *take*:

1 He had a row* with his boss and <u>vented</u> his anger on his wife.
2 The aeroplane <u>left the ground</u> smoothly.
3 Your son <u>resembles</u> you in many ways.
4 If I were you I would <u>employ</u> more workers and finish the job quickly.
5 Don't let youself be <u>deceived</u> by appearances.
6 Philip is very popular with his classmates because he is clever at <u>mimicking</u> the teachers.
7 I hope I haven't <u>occupied</u> too much of your time.
8 Her skirt was too loose and had to be <u>made narrower.</u>
9 I was so <u>surprised</u> by his reply that I couldn't say a word.
10 The newsreporters <u>recorded</u> the main points of the President's speech.
11 That large company has <u>assumed control of</u> many smaller ones.
12 The children <u>liked</u> the new maid immediately.

# THINK

**think about**         reflect upon
1 *vt insep*            *pensar en*

                        I *have been thinking about* this all week, but I still can't
                        understand it.
                        I *thought about* you all day, wondering what had hap-
                        pened to you.

**think about**         consider; contemplate
2 *vt insep*            *considerar; meditar*

                        Give me just a few more days *to think about* your offer.
                        I shall have *to think about* it carefully before I can give you
                        a definite answer.
                        He *is thinking about* leaving his job and starting his own
                        business.

**think about**         have an opinion about
3 *vt insep*            *pensar de; opinar de*

                        She doesn't seem to care what other people *think*
                        about her.
                        Could you just look through this article and tell me
                        what you *think about* it?

| | |
|---|---|
| **think back**<br>*vi* | turn the mind to past events<br>*volverse atrás; pensar (en un tiempo pasado)* |

He *thought back* and tried to remember where he had seen that face before.
Seeing those photographs made me *think back* to my early days in the army.

| | |
|---|---|
| **think of**<br>1 *vt insep* | remember; recall<br>*acordarse de; recordar* |

Can you *think of* the Greek word for 'submarine'*?
I know who you mean, but I can't *think of* his name at the moment.
You *will think of* me sometimes, won't you?

| | |
|---|---|
| **think of**<br>2 *vt insep* | consider; take into account<br>*pensar en; tener en cuenta* |

He has his wife and family *to think of*.
She never *thinks of* anyone but herself.
I have other things *to think of*, you know!

| | |
|---|---|
| **think of**<br>3 *vt insep* | plan to; contemplate<br>*pensar; ocurrírsele a uno hacer* |

Where *are* you *thinking of* going for your holidays this summer?
I *did think of* phoning you at that late hour, but thought you might not like it.
She *would* never *think of* marrying a horrible man like him.

| | |
|---|---|
| **think of**<br>4 *vt insep* | have an opinion of<br>*pensar; estimar; opinar* |

What *do* you *think of* Omar Sharif as an actor?
I don't *think* much *of* the so-called 'modern' art.
His poetry *is* well *thought of* by the critics.

| | |
|---|---|
| **think of**<br>5 *vt insep* | find; suggest<br>*ocurrírsele a uno; pensar* |

We must *think of* some plan to get out of this place.
That's the only decent restaurant I can *think of* at the moment.

| | |
|---|---|
| **think of** | imagine |
| 6 *vt insep* | *imaginar; fijarse* |

*Think of* all the time you have wasted!
Just *think of* the cost of a project like that!

| | |
|---|---|
| **think out** | plan by careful thinking |
| *vt sep* | *idear; estudiar; planear.* |

The assassin's* escape route *had been* carefully *thought out*.
The scheme seems *to be* well *thought out*.

| | |
|---|---|
| **think over** | consider at length |
| *vt sep* | *considerar; reflexionar sobre* |

We need a couple of days *to think over* your suggestions before we commit ourselves.
Please *think* this matter *over* and let me know your answer by Friday.

| | |
|---|---|
| **think up** | invent; concoct |
| *vt sep* | *inventar; idear* |

Can't you *think up* some excuse to give him?
It's not always easy *to think up* original ideas.


*EXERCISE 40*

Fill in the blank spaces with the correct prepositions or particles:

1 Can you think ... the name of the first astronaut* to land on the moon?
2 Just think ... all the money the government is spending on armament*.
3 She is very quick at thinking ... stories.
4 I don't know what to think ... this whole damned thing.
5 Your teachers obviously think very highly ... you.
6 The plot to depose* the king had been thoroughly thought ... by the conspirators*.
7 Think it ... and let me know what you decide.
8 Now think ..., Mrs Atkings, and see if you can remember anything at all that might help us find the murderer.
9 What were you thinking ... when I came in?
10 I just couldn't think ... harming that poor old lady.

153

# THROW

**throw about**
*vt sep\**

throw here and there; scatter
*tirar; derrochar (dinero)*

You mustn't *throw* litter *about* in the park.
He *is throwing* his money *about* like a madman.

**throw away**
1 *vt sep*

discard; dispose of
*tirar; desechar*

We should *throw away* this table and buy a new one.
Don't *throw* those boxes *away*; they may come in handy\* one day.

**throw away**
2 *vt sep*

let slip; miss
*perder; desperdiciar*

You should never *have thrown away* such a good proposition\*.
She had a marvellous opportunity to become an actress, but she *threw* it *away*.

**throw in**
1 *vt insep*

include without extra charge
*dar gratis; incluir*

If you buy the house, we'll *throw in* the carpets.
He said I could have the scooter for only £30, with the helmet\* *thrown in*.

**throw in**
2 *vt sep*

interject
*intercalar; insertar*

He kept *throwing in* silly comments in spite of the chairman's warnings.

**throw off**
1 *vt sep*

remove hurriedly
*quitarse (de prisa)*

She *threw off* her coat and shoes and lay down on the sofa.

**throw off**
2 *vt insep*

get rid of; free oneself from
*quitarse; deshacerse de*

I don't seem to be able *to throw off* this wretched cold.
*Throwing off* all sense of pride, she begged him to marry her.
It is about time we *threw off* the yoke* of imperialism.

**throw out**
1 *vt sep*

expel; remove forcibly
*echar; poner de patitas en la calle; expulsar (del colegio, etc)*

The landlord threatened *to throw* her *out* if she didn't pay the rent.
He *has been thrown out* of college for bad conduct.

**throw out**
2 *vt insep*

emit; produce
*emitir; producir*

Coal fires don't always *throw out* much heat.
This small lamp *throws out* a very strong light.

**throw out**
3 *vt sep*

reject
*rechazar*

The board of directors are inclined *to throw out* any proposals put forward by us.
The Bill *was thrown out* by a majority of 30 votes.

**throw out**
4 *vt sep*

= throw away (1)

**throw over**
*vt sep*

abandon; desert; forsake
*romper con; dar calabazas a; dejar a*

She *threw over* her old friends when she won a fortune on the pools.
She *has thrown* her lover *over* for someone wealthier.

**throw up**
1 *vi, vt sep*

vomit; bring up
*vomitar; devolver*

I can't eat anything: I feel like *throwing up*.
The sick child kept *throwing up* her food.

155

**throw up**   abandon; give up
2 *vt sep*   *abandonar; renunciar a*

She *threw up* her job to look after her ailing father.
He *threw up* a promising career in the Foreign* Office
to become a free-lance* photographer.

EXERCISE 41

Fill in the blank spaces with the correct prepositions or particles:

1 Keep quiet, Sally, or I'll throw you . . . .
2 He threw . . . a good chance to compete in the Olympic Games.
3 He wouldn't stop throwing . . . all kinds of facetious* remarks.
4 Don't throw your books . . . in the room; the place looks terribly untidy.
5 I'll throw . . . two new tyres if you decide to buy the car.
6 That radiator doesn't throw . . . a lot of heat.
7 It would be foolish of you to throw . . . such a good job.
8 It took me more than a week to throw . . . that flu I had.
9 He threatened to kill his mistress if she threw him . . . .
10 He was terribly drunk and threw . . . everything he had eaten.

# TURN

**turn against**   (cause to) become hostile to
*vi, vt sep**   *predisponerle a uno en contra de*

He had a strong feeling that all his friends *were turning
against* him.
I will never forgive her for *turning* my own son *against* me.

**turn (a) round**   face in the opposite direction
*vi*   *dar(se) la vuelta*

She dared not *turn round* to see who was following her
in the dark.

**turn away**   look in a different direction
1 *vi*   *volver la cara; apartar la mirada*

She *turned away* in horror at the sight of her but-
chered husband.

156

| | |
|---|---|
| **turn away**<br>2 *vt sep* | refuse admission or help to sb.<br>*rechazar* |
| | These organizations seldom *turn away* anyone who is in dire\* need of help.<br>As all tickets were sold out, many people had *to be turned away.*<br>I really hate *to turn* beggars *away*. |
| **turn back**<br>1 *vi, vt sep* | (cause to) go back<br>*(a) volverse atrás; (b) hacer volver o retroceder* |
| | Don't you think we should *turn back* now before the storm gets any worse?<br>The guards *turned* us *back* at the main gate.<br>They *turned* their car *back* and headed for safety. |
| **turn back**<br>2 *vt sep* | fold back<br>*doblar; plegar* |
| | She *turned back* the corner of the page to mark her place in the book. |
| **turn down**<br>1 *vt sep* | fold down<br>*doblar* |
| | I wish you would stop this habit of *turning down* the pages of the book. |
| **turn down**<br>2 *vt sep* | lessen the intensity of; lower<br>*bajar* |
| | Don't forget *to turn down* the gas when the milk boils.<br>She *turned* the oil lamp *down*. |
| **turn down**<br>3 *vt sep* | refuse; reject<br>*rechazar; no aceptar* |
| | He did apply for that post, but they *turned* him *down*.<br>She *turned down* the job because it was badly paid.<br>His first book *was turned down* by a number of publishers. |

157

**turn in**
1 *vi*

go to bed
*acostarse; irse a la cama*

It was close upon midnight when we *turned in*.
It's time the children *were turning in*.

**turn in**
2 *vt sep*

surrender to the police
*entregar (a la policía)*

If we don't *turn* him *in* this time, the chances are he'll go on breaking the law.
She begged me not *to turn* her *in* and promised never to steal again.

**turn inside out**
*vt sep**

reverse the sides; search thoroughly
*(a) volver al revés; (b) registrar de arriba abajo*

The strong wind *turned* her umbrella *inside out*.
The police *turned* the place *inside out* in search of the murder weapon.

**turn into**
*vi, vt sep**

become; convert into
*transformar(se); convertir(se)*

A caterpillar* ultimately *turns into* a butterfly or a moth.
Jesus is said *to have turned* water *into* wine.
We *are going to turn* the basement into a workshop.

**turn off**
1 *vi, vt insep*

branch off; change direction
*deviarse (de su camino)*

This is where the road to Lancaster *turns off*.
*Turn off* (the motorway) at the next exit.

**turn off**
2 *vt sep*

stop the flow of; switch off
*cerrar (un grifo); apagar (la luz)*

You forgot *to turn off* the water in the bathroom.
Remember *to turn* the lights *off* before you go to bed.

**turn off**
3 *vt sep**

cause to lose interest in
*resultar molesto; molestar*

This kind of music really *turns* me *off*.

| | |
|---|---|
| **turn on**<br>1 *vt sep* | start the flow of; switch on<br>*encender; poner* |
| | I'*ll turn on* the heater for a few minutes, if you don't mind.<br>Please *turn* the oven *on*; I'm going to bake some cakes. |
| **turn on**<br>2 *vt sep*\* | excite; stimulate<br>*entusiasmar; excitar* |
| | I think she is a great singer; she really *turns* the audience *on*.<br>That jazz sure *turns* me *on*, man! |
| **turn on**<br>3 *vt insep* | depend on<br>*depender de* |
| | The success of these talks *turns on* the willingness of both sides to make considerable concessions\*. |
| **turn on**<br>4 *vt insep* | attack<br>*atacar; agredir* |
| | The dog *turned on* the postman and bit him in the thigh. |
| **turn out**<br>1 *vi* | assemble; gather<br>*salir a la calle; reunirse* |
| | The whole village *turned out* to welcome the Queen.<br>In spite of the cold weather, thousands of people *turned out* to see the Grand\* National. |
| **turn out**<br>2 *vi* | prove to be; transpire<br>*resultar ser; resultar que* |
| | He *turned out* to be a thoroughly dishonest person.<br>The project *turned out* (to be) a complete failure.<br>It *turned out* that he was a Russian spy. |
| **turn out**<br>3 *vt sep* | evict; expel<br>*echar; poner de patitas en la calle* |
| | Her landlord *turned* her *out* for not paying the rent.<br>*Turn* those children *out* of my study, will you? |

159

| | |
|---|---|
| **turn out**<br>4 *vt sep* | clean thoroughly; empty<br>*arreglar; limpiar (una habitación); vaciar (el bolsillo)* |
| | My mother *turns out* the bedrooms once a week.<br>He *turned* his pockets *out* in search of his train ticket. |
| **turn out**<br>5 *vt sep* | extinguish<br>*apagar* |
| | Don't forget *to turn out* the lights before you go out. |
| **turn over**<br>1 *vi* | capsize; overturn<br>*volcar(se); zozobrar (barcos)* |
| | The small rowing-boat *turned over* in the gale.<br>The car hit a lamp-post and *turned over*. |
| **turn over**<br>2 *vi, vt sep* | change sides; invert<br>*(a) volver; poner al revés; (b) revolverse (en la cama)* |
| | He couldn't sleep last night and kept *turning over* in bed.<br>Nobody could *turn over* that big stone.<br>Will you help me *turn* the mattress *over*, please? |
| **turn over**<br>3 *vt insep* | do business to the amount of<br>*hacer negocios por valor de* |
| | We *turned over* no less than a million pounds last year. |
| **turn over**<br>4 *vt sep* | deliver; hand over<br>*entregar* |
| | They *turned* the escaped prisoner *over* to the police.<br>You did the right thing in *turning* him *over* to the authorities. |
| **turn to**<br>*vt insep* | go to (for help, advice, etc.)<br>*recurrir a; acudir a uno (a pedir ayuda)* |
| | She has no one *to turn to* for advice, poor thing!<br>He always *turns to* me when he is in trouble. |

**turn up**
1 *vi*

arrive; come
*llegar; venir; asistir*

I waited for him for nearly one hour, but he did not *turn up*.
Only half the members *turned up* at last night's meeting.

**turn up**
2 *vi*

come to light; be found
*volver a aparecer; aparecer*

These things always *turn up* when you don't need them.
Please don't worry about my lighter; it'*ll turn up* eventually.

**turn up**
3 *vi*

happen; occur
*ocurrir; surgir*

If anything *turns up*, I'll let you know.
Something is bound *to turn up* sooner or later.

**turn up**
4 *vt sep*

cause to face upwards
*subirse (el cuello del abrigo); hacer ver (una carta)*

She *turned up* the collar of her coat against the cold wind.

**turn up**
5 *vt sep*

find; discover
*descubrir; encontrar*

You can always *turn up* his address in the telephone directory.
We *have turned up* some information that may interest you.

**turn up**
6 *vt sep*

increase the intensity of (cf: *turn down*)
*poner mas fuerte (véase TURN DOWN)*

Will you *turn up* the radio, John? I can hardly hear a thing.
*Turn up* the gas just a little bit.

161

| turn upside | invert; search thoroughly |
| down | *(a) invertir; poner al revés; (b) poner un sitio patas arriba* |
| vt sep* | |

You've *turned* the painting *upside down*, haven't you?
He *turned* the whole place *upside down*, looking for his boots.

## EXERCISES 42

**A** Fill in the blank spaces with the correct prepositions or particles. In some examples more than one answer is possible:

1 I haven't found a job yet, but I hope something will turn ... soon.
2 Turn your collar ... ; it's sticking up at the back.
3 Do you mind turning ... the wireless? It's making too much noise.
4 He never lets down anyone who turns ... him for help.
5 That shop turns ... something like a thousand pounds a day.
6 The oil tanker* caught fire and turned ... an inferno*.
7 Turn ... the television if you are not watching it.
8 Thieves broke into the shop and turned everything ... ... ...
9 Turn ... the light, please; it's getting dark in here.
10 A large crowd turned ... to welcome the president.

**B** Replace the underlined words with phrasal verbs containing *turn*:

1 We went to bed rather late last night.
2 The small boat capsized in the storm.
3 A lot of people had to be refused admission to the concert-hall.
4 We agreed to be there at eight, but he arrived one hour later.
5 The bull attacked the matador and knocked him senseless.
6 The exam proved to be much easier than we had expected.
7 Everything depends on what happens next.
8 The director refused his request for a transfer to headquarters*.
9 He was expelled from the club because he did not have a membership card.

# WEAR

| wear away | (cause to) disappear or become thin through friction |
| *vi, vt sep* | etc. |
| | *desgastar(se); gastar(se)* |

The inscription* on the monument *has worn away* and can scarcely be read.
The waves *had worn away* the cliffs.
Wind and rain *have worn* these rocks *away*.

| | |
|---|---|
| **wear down**<br>1 *vi, vt sep* | (cause to) become smaller by rubbing or use<br>*desgastar(se); gastar(se)*<br><br>The heels of your shoes *are* quickly *wearing down*.<br>The heels of your shoes *are* badly *worn down*.<br>These rough roads *will* soon *wear down* the tyres of your car. |
| **wear down**<br>2 *vt sep* | weaken by constant pressure or attack<br>*cansar; agotar*<br><br>They have at last succeeded in *wearing down* the opposition.<br>The two boxers were trying *to wear* each other *down*. |
| **wear off**<br>*vi* | disappear; pass away<br>*desaparecer; pasar*<br><br>The public will forget all about this incident as soon as the novelty* *wears off*.<br>I'm glad your headache *is wearing off*. |
| **wear on**<br>*vi* | pass slowly or tediously<br>*pasar; transcurrir*<br><br>As the day *wore on*, she became more and more anxious.<br>Several months *wore on* and nothing was heard of him. |
| **wear out**<br>1 *vi, vt sep* | (cause to) become useless through wear<br>*romperse con el uso; desgastar(se)*<br><br>Children's shoes *wear out* very quickly.<br>Most of the machines in this factory *are wearing out*.<br>Children *wear out* their shoes very quickly.<br>This old jacket *is* almost *worn out*. |
| **wear out**<br>2 *vt sep* | exhaust; tire out<br>*agotarse; cansarse*<br><br>I don't want you *to wear* yourself *out* like that.<br>What's the matter, Nick? You look utterly *worn out*. |

163

*EXERCISE 43*

Fill in the blank spaces with the correct prepositions or particles:

1 She was completely worn ... after a long, busy day.
2 Everyone was growing restless as the evening wore ... and nothing happened.
3 Cheap clothes do not necessarily wear ... more quickly than expensive ones.
4 Her shyness will probably wear ... when she gets to know you better.
5 You'll have to wear this coat ... before I can buy you a new one.
6 You should sharpen your pencil; the point is quite worn ....
7 The feet of so many tourists had worn ... the steps.
8 We must wear ... the enemy's resistance at all costs.

# WORK

| | |
|---|---|
| **work at**<br>*vt insep* | apply oneself to; be busy at<br>*(a) trabajar en; estar ocupado en; (b) aplicarse a* |

You've got *to work at* your German if you want to have a chance of passing the exam.
I *have been working at* this essay all week.

| | |
|---|---|
| **work in (to)**<br>*vt sep* | introduce<br>*introducir* |

His lectures wouldn't be so dull if he could *work in* a bit of humour.
He always manages *to work* politics *into* the conversation.

| | |
|---|---|
| **work off**<br>*vt sep* | get rid of; vent<br>*desahogarse; quitarse; deshacerse de* |

By this time next year I *will have worked off* all my debts.
She *worked off* her anger on the poor dog.

| | |
|---|---|
| **work on**<br>1 *vt insep* | be engaged in<br>*trabajar en; dedicarse a* |

We *are working on* a slightly different project at present.
What exactly *is* he *working on* for his doctorate?

**work on**
2 *vt insep*

seek to persuade or influence sb.
*tratar de persuadir a uno*

He won't let me do it unless you *work on* him.
I don't promise you anything, but I shall certainly *work on* him.

**work out**
1 *vi*

develop in a certain way
*salir (bien o mal); resultar*

Things did not quite *work out* the way we had hoped.
Everything *worked out* all right in the end.

**work out**
2 *vi*

train oneself physically
*entrenarse*

The athletes *worked out* for five hours a day before the Olympics.

**work out**
3 *vi, vt sep*

estimate; calculate
*calcular*

We *worked out* that it would cost £300 to instal a central-heating system.
I'*ll have to work out* the cost of this trip to see if we can afford it.

**work out**
4 *vt sep*

solve
*resolver; solucionar*

I can't *work out* these difficult equations*.
Have you *worked out* this puzzle yet?

**work out**
5 *vt sep*

devise; plan
*elaborar; idear*

I think we ought to wait until we *have worked out* a plan of campaign.
It seems to be a well *worked-out* scheme.

**work out**
6 *vt sep*

exhaust (a mine)
*agotar (una mina)*

Those coalmines are now completely *worked out*.

165

| | |
|---|---|
| **work out at**<br>*v t insep* | amount to<br>*sumar; llegar a; ascender a* |

His fees* *work out at* forty pounds a day.
What does your share of the profits *work out at*?

| | |
|---|---|
| **work up**<br>1 *vt sep* | arouse; excite<br>*excitar; excitarse* |

The speaker *was working up* the crowd into an absolute frenzy*.
Oh, you *do work* yourself *up* over nothing.
What's she so *worked up* about?

| | |
|---|---|
| **work up**<br>2 *vt sep* | develop; build up<br>*desarrollar* |

My brother and I *worked up* the business from nothing.
I might try *to work up* these notes into a small book.

| | |
|---|---|
| **work up**<br>3 *vt sep* | stimulate; arouse<br>*fomentar; estimular* |

So far we haven't been able *to work up* any enthusiasm for the scheme.
A brisk walk in the park *will work up* your appetite.

| | |
|---|---|
| **work up to**<br>1 *vt insep* | rise gradually to<br>*llegar poco a poco a* |

The story *works up to* a thrilling climax.

| | |
|---|---|
| **work up to**<br>2 *vt insep* | prepare the way for<br>*preparar el terreno para* |

What exactly *are* you *working up to*?

*EXERCISE 44*
Use synonyms in place of the underlined phrasal verbs:

1 He seems to be fond of <u>working</u> quotations* <u>into</u> his speeches.
2 Please don't <u>work</u> your <u>bad temper off</u> on me.
3 He certainly knows how to <u>work up</u> an audience.
4 Skiing* isn't easy; you've got to <u>work at</u> it.
5 Can you <u>work out</u> how long it will take us to get to Hull from here?

6 He is now working on a new novel.
7 You should be able to work out this problem in a couple of minutes.
8 Scientists have recently worked out a new method of measuring the depths of the oceans.
9 We have worked up a great deal of interest in your campaign.
10 The bill works out at five pounds each.

# ENGLISH – SPANISH GLOSSARY

The page reference given indicates the place where the word first occurs in the text. Each word translated in the glossary is marked with an asterisk (*) in the text.

La referencia de página indica el sitio donde la palabra aparece por primera vez en el texto. Cada palabra traducida en el glosario está marcada con un asterisco en el texto.

| | |
|---|---|
| abbreviation, p. 142 | *abreviatura* |
| abide by, p. 10 | *atenerse a; cumplir* |
| abolition, p. 12 | *abolición; anulación* |
| abortive, p. 29 | *fracasado; ineficaz; estéril* |
| accomplish, p. 96 | *realizar; llevar a cabo* |
| accumulate, p. 34 | *amontonar; contraer* |
| acquaintances, p. 37 | *amigos; conocidos* |
| A.D. (Anno Domini), p. 142 | *D.C. (Después de Cristo)* |
| adequate, p. 53 | *suficiente* |
| affair, p. 54 | *plan; relación amorosa; lío (fam.)* |
| agenda, p. 79 | *orden del día* |
| ailment, p. 84 | *enfermedad* |
| air-raid, p. 63 | *ataque aéreo* |
| allegations, p. 28 | *aseveraciones; alegaciones* |
| ammunition, p. 62 | *municiones* |
| ancestor, p. 84 | *antepasado* |
| annual, p. 126 | *anual; por año* |
| antagonize, p. 85 | *provocar; enemistarse con* |
| Antarctic, p. 134 | *Antártida* |
| anticipate, p. 52 | *prever; esperar* |

| | |
|---|---|
| appendix, p. 148 | *apéndice* |
| applause, p. 68 | *aplausos; aprobación* |
| application, p. 62 | *solicitud; instancia* |
| appreciably, p. 51 | *perceptiblemente* |
| armament, p. 153 | *armamento* |
| arrogant, p. 150 | *arrogante; soberbio* |
| arthritis, p. 83 | *artritis* |
| artillery, p. 27 | *artillería* |
| assassin, p. 153 | *asesino* |
| assassination, p. 65 | *asesinato* |
| assault, p. 116 | *agredir; atacar* |
| astronaut, p. 153 | *astronauta* |
| athlete, p. 31 | *atleta* |
| attic, p. 48 | *desván; buhardilla* |
| auctioneer, p. 86 | *subastador* |
| auditor, p. 72 | *interventor* |
| authorities, p. 75 | *autoridades* |

| | |
|---|---|
| back-bencher, p. 28 | *diputado (que no es ministro)* |
| ban, p. 117 | *prohibición* |
| bandit, p. 53 | *bandido* |
| bank on, p. 52 | *contar con* |
| bankrupt, p. 78 | *insolvente; en bancarrota* |
| barbed wire, p. 83 | *alambre de espino* |
| beleaguered, p. 79 | *sitiado; asediado* |
| benefactor, p. 122 | *bienhechor; padrino* |
| bereavement, p. 17 | *aflicción (por la muerte de un pariente)* |
| besieged, p. 62 | *sitiado; asediado* |
| bickering, p. 52 | *riñas; peleas* |

| | |
|---|---|
| Bill, p. 24 | *proyecto de ley* |
| binoculars, p. 100 | *gemelos; prismáticos* |
| blackmail, p. 62 | *chantaje* |
| blinds, p. 111 | *persianas* |
| blood donor, p. 76 | *donador de sangre* |
| book, p. 132 | *reservar* |
| book-keeper, p. 31 | *contable* |
| brag, p. 145 | *jactarse; fanfarronear* |
| brochure, p. 75 | *folleto* |
| budget, p. 129 | *presupuesto* |
| building society, p. 110 | *sociedad inmobiliaria* |
| bully, p. 143 | *tirano; matón* |
| burglar, p. 20 | *ladrón* |
| butler, p. 137 | *mayordomo* |
| campaign, p. 61 | *campaña* |
| cancer, p. 135 | *cáncer* |
| candidate, p. 48 | *candidato; opositor* |
| candidate, p. 125 | *candidato* |
| capital, p. 32 | *capital* |
| capital punishment, p. 23 | *pena de muerte* |
| capsize, p. 18 | *zozobrar; volcarse* |
| cargo, p. 132 | *carga; cargamento* |
| casualties, p. 63 | *víctimas; muertes* |
| caterpillar, p. 158 | *oruga* |
| cause, p. 89 | *causa* |
| challenger, p. 87 | *contrincante* |
| champion, p. 87 | *campeón* |
| charitable foundations, p. 62 | *sociedades benéficas* |
| charity, p. 65 | *sociedad benéfica* |

171

| | |
|---|---|
| chess, p. 147 | *ajedrez* |
| cholera, p. 21 | *cólera* |
| Christmas, p. 67 | *Navidad* |
| club, p. 132 | *porra* |
| commandos, p. 18 | *comando* |
| commission, p. 136 | *comisión* |
| commit suicide, p. 41 | *suicidarse* |
| committee, p. 27 | *comisión; consejo; comité* |
| commute, p. 133 | *conmutar* |
| competition, p. 31 | *concurso* |
| comply with, p. 10 | *conformarse con; obedecer* |
| computer, p. 47 | *computador; ordenador* |
| | |
| concessions, p. 159 | *concesiones* |
| conservative, p. 33 | *conservador* |
| conspirator, p. 153 | *conspirador* |
| consultation, p. 28 | *consulta* |
| contemporary, p. 141 | *contemporáneo* |
| contest, p. 70 | *concurso* |
| controversy, p. 134 | *controversia* |
| convert, p. 145 | *convertir; transformar* |
| convict, p. 58 | *presidiario; preso* |
| convoy, p. 53 | *convoy* |
| corporal punishment, p. 27 | *castigo corporal* |
| corpse, p. 90 | *cadáver* |
| corruption, p. 28 | *corrupción* |
| crisis (pl. crises), p. 41 | *crisis* |
| critic, p. 12 | *crítico* |
| crook, p. 91 | *criminal* |
| culprit, p. 95 | *culpable* |

| | |
|---|---|
| cultivation, p. 27 | *cultivo* |
| customs officer, p. 72 | *aduanero* |
| | |
| daffodil, p. 41 | *narciso trompón* |
| death penalty, p. 12 | *pena de muerte* |
| debate, p. 49 | *debate; discusión* |
| debris, p. 34 | *escombros* |
| defective, p. 29 | *defectuoso* |
| deficit, p. 105 | *déficit* |
| delegation, p. 15 | *delegación* |
| dentist, p. 59 | *dentista* |
| depose, p. 153 | *deponer* |
| depression, p. 89 | *depresión; crisis* |
| derelict, p. 112 | *abandonado* |
| destination, p. 25 | *destino; paradero* |
| destiny, p. 25 | *destino* |
| deteriorate, p. 44 | *empeorar; deteriorar* |
| diagnosis, p. 13 | *diagnóstico* |
| diligence, p. 61 | *diligencia* |
| dire, p. 157 | *extremado* |
| disabled, p. 61 | *minusválido* |
| disarray, p. 50 | *confusión; desorden* |
| disaster, p. 63 | *desastre* |
| discretion, p. 96 | *discreción* |
| dissertation, p. 128 | *tesis; disertación* |
| divorce, p. 50 | *divorciarse* |
| dock, p. 132 | *puerto; muelle* |
| dogged, p. 21 | *obstinado; tenaz* |
| dogged, p. 32 | *obstinado* |
| draft dodger, p. 37 | *el que evade al servicio militar; desertor* |

| | |
|---|---|
| draught, p. 83 | *corriente de aire* |
| drench, p. 38 | *mojar(se)* |
| drive, p. 98 | *ambición; energía* |
| drought, p. 24 | *sequía* |
| dull-witted, p. 146 | *torpe* |
| | |
| earthquake, p. 45 | *terremoto* |
| Easter, p. 22 | *Pascua de Resurrección* |
| election, p. 41 | *elección* |
| electorate, p. 115 | *electorado* |
| emergency, p. 24 | *emergencia; crisis; urgencia* |
| encyclopaedia, p. 27 | *enciclopedia* |
| enterprise, p. 32 | *empresa* |
| enthusiasm, p. 30 | *entusiasmo* |
| epidemic, p. 21 | *epidemia* |
| equation, p. 165 | *ecuación* |
| estimate, p. 15 | *cálculo* |
| evidence. p. 11 | *pruebas* |
| evidence. p. 45 | *declaración; testimonio* |
| expedition, p. 134 | *expedición* |
| expenditure, p. 78 | *gastos* |
| explorer, p. 40 | *explorador* |
| extension. p. 123 | *extensión* |
| | |
| facetious, p. 156 | *gracioso* |
| fanatic, p. 47 | *fanático* |
| fancy-dress ball, p. 61 | *baile de disfraces.* |
| fees, p. 73 | *precios; cuotas* |
| fees, p. 166 | *honorarios* |
| feign, p. 58 | *fingir(se)* |

174

| | |
|---|---|
| heiress, p. 35 | *heredera* |
| helmet, p. 154 | *casco* |
| hitch, p. 71 | *problema; dificultad* |
| Home Secretary, p. 28 | *Ministro del Interior* |
| hooligan, p. 137 | *gamberro* |
| hostage, p. 42 | *rehén* |
| hot-dog, p. 136 | *perro caliente* |
| hygienic, p. 103 | *higiénico* |
| | |
| illicit, p. 25 | *ilícito* |
| impertinence, p. 122 | *insolencia; impertenencia* |
| impostor, p. 138 | *impostor* |
| impression , p. 126 | *tirada; edición* |
| impudence, p. 17 | *insolencia* |
| indecent exposure, p. 126 | *exhibicionismo* |
| indignation, p. 82 | *indignación* |
| indispensable, p. 124 | *imprescindible* |
| inferno, p. 162 | *infierno* |
| inflation, p. 14 | *inflación* |
| infidelity, p. 109 | *infidelidad* |
| infinite, p. 41 | *infinito; enorme* |
| initiative, p. 98 | *iniciativa* |
| inquiry, p. 28 | *investigación* |
| inscription, p. 162 | *inscripción* |
| instalments, p. 50 | *(pago a) plazos/letras* |
| interest, p. 109 | *interés* |
| intimidation, p. 141 | *intimidación* |
| intruder, p. 69 | *intruso* |
| investment, p. 24 | *inversión* |

| | |
|---|---|
| invigilator, p. 63 | *vigilante* |
| item, p. 52 | *artículo; cosa* |
| item, p. 79 | *asunto* |
| item, p. 72 | *cosa* |
| jockey, p. 86 | *jockey* |
| jubilant, p. 81 | *jubiloso* |
| jury, p. 24 | *jurado* |
| kidnap, p. 35 | *secuestrar; raptar* |
| laughing stock, p. 56 | *hazmerreir* |
| lay-by. p. 112 | *lugar donde se puede aparcar* |
| leaflet, p. 63 | *folleto* |
| League of Nations, p. 137 | *Sociedad de Naciones* |
| leak, spring a —, p. 69 | *hacer agua* |
| leeway, p. 105 | *trabajo/tiempo a recuperar* |
| legend, p. 75 | *leyenda* |
| letter, to the —, p. 32 | *exactamente; al pie de la letra* |
| lodger, p. 31 | *huésped* |
| loot, p. 22 | *saquear* |
| lot, a bad —, p. 150 | *mala gente* |
| magistrate, p. 94 | *magistrado; juez* |
| mahogany, p. 86 | *caoba* |
| maiden voyage, p. 69 | *viaje inaugural* |
| maintenance, p. 19 | *mantenimiento* |
| malnutrition, p. 20 | *desnutrición* |
| manifesto, p. 115 | *manifiesto* |

| | |
|---|---|
| Marathon, p. 50 | *maratón* |
| matador, p. 69 | *matador de toros* |
| measures, p. 23 | *medidas* |
| minutes, p. 30 | *acta; actas* |
| mischief, p. 15 | *daño; travesura* |
| missile, p. 23 | *mísil; proyectil* |
| moaning, p. 43 | *quejas; protestas* |
| moth, p. 90 | *polilla* |
| motion, p. 137 | *moción; proposición* |
| M.P. (Member of Parliament), p. 23 | *diputado; miembro del parlamento* |
| municipal, p. 143 | *municipal* |

| | |
|---|---|
| naivety, p. 46 | *sencillez; ingenuidad* |
| napping, catch sb. —, p. 41 | *coger a uno desprevenido* |
| nationalization, p. 19 | *nacionalización* |
| neck, stick one's — out, p. 147 | *arriesgarse; atreverse* |
| negotiations, p. 19 | *negociaciónes* |
| nomads, p. 51 | *nómadas* |
| nonsense, p. 43 | *tonterías* |
| novelty, p. 163 | *novedad* |
| nudity, p. 9 | *desnudez* |

| | |
|---|---|
| obstacle, p. 129 | *obstáculo* |
| obstinate, p. 143 | *obstinado; terco* |
| office, p. 39 | *cargo; oficio* |
| Opposition leader, p. 78 | *jefe de la oposición* |
| opponent, p. 88 | *contrincante; adversario* |
| ordeal, p. 32 | *prueba; experiencia* |
| ornithology, p. 41 | *ornitología* |
| outdated, p. 47 | *anticuado; pasado de moda* |

178

| | |
|---|---|
| outlaw, p. 149 | *forajido* |
| outrageous, p. 80 | *escandaloso* |
| outstanding, p. 110 | *a pagar; por pagar (de una deuda)* |
| overdue, p. 30 | *atrasado* |

| | |
|---|---|
| package tour, p. 146 | *viaje organizado* |
| panic, p. 39 | *pánico* |
| patent, p. 150 | *patente* |
| penalize, p. 10 | *castigar; penalizar* |
| permissive society, p. 78 | *sociedad permisiva* |
| petty cash, p. 52 | *dinero para gastos menores* |
| petty thief, p. 94 | *ladrón* |
| pincers, p. 113 | *tenazas* |
| pitch, p. 30 | *campo* |
| plead with, p. 64 | *rogar* |
| pneumonia, p. 25 | *pulmonía* |
| poke, p. 71 | *atizar; remover* |
| pools, p. 82 | *quinielas* |
| pop star, p. 101 | *cantante pop* |
| prejudices, p. 91 | *prejuicios* |
| premier, p. 75 | *primer ministro* |
| premises, p. 130 | *local; casa; tienda* |
| prescription, p. 105 | *receta* |
| prey, p. 16 | *presa; víctima* |
| procession, p. 29 | *desfile* |
| procession, p. 109 | *cortejo fúnebre* |
| project, p. 53 | *proyecto* |
| promotion, p. 17 | *promoción; ascenso* |
| proposal, p. 9 | *propuesta; idea* |

| | |
|---|---|
| proposition, p. 154 | *propuesta; proposición* |
| provisions, p. 79 | *provisiones; víveres* |
| provocative, p. 82 | *provocador; provocativo* |
| quid, p. 137 | *libra (esterlina)* |
| quotation, p. 166 | *cita* |
| ransack, p. 20 | *saquear* |
| rashness, p. 110 | *temeridad* |
| rebellion, p. 117 | *rebelión* |
| rebellious, p. 85 | *rebelde* |
| reconciliation, p. 23 | *(re)conciliación* |
| reconnaissance, p. 27 | *reconocimiento* |
| refinery, p. 18 | *refinería* |
| reform, p. 24 | *reforma* |
| regiment, p. 43 | *regimiento* |
| reinforcements, p. 79 | *refuerzos* |
| renovate, p. 50 | *renovar* |
| reputation, p. 85 | *reputación; fama* |
| reserved, p. 49 | *reservado* |
| reservist, p. 29 | *reservista* |
| resignation, p. 55 | *dimisión* |
| resort, p. 32 | *lugar de veraneo* |
| resume, p. 19 | *reanudar; continuar* |
| retirement, p. 88 | *jubilación* |
| reviewer, p. 44 | *crítico* |
| revolt, p. 117 | *sublevación* |
| rich, p. 42 | *rico; sabroso* |
| riot, p. 22 | *disturbio* |
| rogue, p. 142 | *gamberro* |

| | |
|---|---|
| row, p. 151 | *bronca; pelea* |
| rumour, p. 54 | *rumor* |
| runway, p. 126 | *pista de aterrizaje* |
| ruthlessly, p. 78 | *implacablemente* |

| | |
|---|---|
| scaffolding, p. 145 | *andamio* |
| scandal, p. 19 | *escándalo* |
| schedule, p. 12 | *plan; horario* |
| scheme, p. 22 | *proyecto* |
| sea, go to —, p. 124 | *hacerse marinero* |
| seamstress, p. 44 | *costurera* |
| sedative, p. 96 | *calmante* |
| sentry, p. 128 | *guardia, centinela* |
| sergeant, p. 18 | *sargento* |
| sex equality, p. 80 | *igualdad de los sexos* |

| | |
|---|---|
| sharp, p. 60 | *en punto* |
| shorthand, p. 98 | *taquigrafía* |
| shrewd, p. 33 | *listo; perspicaz* |
| skid, p. 129 | *derrapar* |
| skiing, p. 166 | *esquí* |
| slump, p. 42 | *depresión; crisis económica* |
| snack, p. 87 | *piscolabis* |
| snobbish, p. 102 | *(e)snob* |

| | |
|---|---|
| sparkling, p. 41 | *brillante* |
| spectator, p. 139 | *espectador* |
| spy, p. 62 | *espía* |
| squalid, p. 27 | *miserable; asqueroso* |
| starvation, p. 139 | *hambre; inanición* |

| | |
|---|---|
| stationary, p. 126 | *estacionario* |
| statistics, p. 20 | *estadísticas* |
| stray, p. 146 | *extraviado* |
| study, p. 83 | *despacho; estudio* |
| stuff, p. 115 | *materia; especialidad* |
| submarine, p. 152 | *submarino* |
| surgeon, p. 41 | *cirujano* |
| surplus, p. 27 | *excedente; exceso* |
| surrender, p. 43 | *rendición* |
| surveyor, p. 100 | *topógrafo; agrimensor* |
| suspect, p. 72 | *sospechoso* |
| synonym, p. 18 | *sinónimo* |

| | |
|---|---|
| tact, p. 28 | *discreción; tacto* |
| tanker, p. 162 | *petrolero* |
| tax evasion, p. 27 | *evasión fiscal* |
| tear-gas, p. 22 | *gas lacrimógeno* |
| teenager, p. 101 | *joven (de 13 a 19 años)* |
| terrorist, p. 134 | *terrorista* |
| thesis, p. 61 | *tesis* |
| through thick and thin, p. 140 | *venga lo que venga; pase lo que pase* |
| tinned, p. 53 | *en lata* |
| tissue, p. 41 | *tejido* |
| Tories, p. 57 | *conservadores* |
| tournament, p. 125 | *torneo* |
| track down, p. 66 | *encontrar; localizar* |
| traffic jam, p. 77 | *embotellamiento* |
| traitor, p. 99 | *traidor* |

| | |
|---|---|
| trespasser, p. 83 | *intruso* |
| trivial, p. 52 | *insignificante* |
| | |
| tropical, p. 9 | *tropical* |
| trophy, p. 32 | *trofeo* |
| truancy, p. 64 | *ausencia (sin permiso); "novillos"* |
| Tube, p. 41 | *Metro* |

| | |
|---|---|
| undertaker, p. 90 | *empresario de pompas fúnebres* |
| unemployment benefit, p. 111 | *subsidio de paro* |
| union, p. 29 | *sindicato* |

| | |
|---|---|
| vacancy, p. 98 | *vacante;* |
| vacuum cleaner, p. 47 | *aspirador* |
| verdict, p. 24 | *veredicto; juicio* |
| virtue, by — of, p. 141 | *en virtud de* |
| vocabulary, p. 74 | *vocabulario* |
| volunteer, p. 77 | *voluntario* |
| vote, p. 135 | *voto* |

| | |
|---|---|
| weed, p. 114 | *mala hierba* |
| will, p. 28 | *testamento* |
| window-sill, p. 97 | *alféizar* |
| wistfully, p. 102 | *tristemente; con melancolía* |
| witness, p. 9 | *testigo* |
| women's lib, p. 80 | *libertad de la mujer* |
| worship, p. 64 | *adoración* |